THE LAZY RUNNER

THE LAZY RUNNER

LAURA FOUNTAIN

pitch

First published by Pitch Publishing, 2015

Pitch Publishing
A2 Yeoman Gate
Yeoman Way
Durrington
BN13 3QZ
www.pitchpublishing.co.uk

A CIP catalogue record is available for this book
from the British Library.

Kindle edition, December 2012

ISBN 978 1-90962-692-8

Typesetting and origination by Pitch Publishing

Printed in Great Britain

Contents

For Mum and Dad, who never told me I couldn't or I shouldn't

Introduction

A FEW years ago I had a vision of myself care-free, running down a beach for the sheer fun of it and looking like I'd just stepped out of a Belinda Carlisle video. I couldn't even run 400 metres back then without gasping and floundering on the floor like a fish out of water, but today that vision is pretty much a reality. I say 'pretty much' because I worry an unhealthy amount about whether I left the oven on to ever be care-free and sweat far too much to look like I came out of a music video, but the running down the beach part for miles and miles is true.

The following pages are an account of how I went from couch potato to marathon-running badass and the lessons I learnt along the way. It is not a marathon training plan, nor is it a 'how to' guide. If you want someone to tell you what you should and shouldn't do, call your mum. This book is an honest account of how difficult it can be to start running but it will, hopefully, show you how rewarding it can be if you stick with it. It will also give you practical tips to help make your journey to becoming a runner easier, things that I've often learnt the hard way.

There are lots of great books, websites and magazines written by Olympic athletes and ultra-clever science folk out there, with training plans you can follow and scientific information on how to train effectively. However, if you want to hear from someone whose only form of exercise for the first 26 years of her life was drunk dancing in sweaty nightclubs, but who ended up with five marathon finishers' t-shirts in her cupboard, then I am that person and this is the book for you. I may not have ever finished first in a race or broken any records, but I do know how difficult it can be to start running, how frustrating it can be when you feel you're not getting any better and how much it can hurt just trying to run that first mile.

I'm also the master of excuses. So if you've got an excuse for not running today, tomorrow or yesterday, I've used it and if you've encountered an obstacle I've been there too – and I've got an answer to both of them. But I genuinely believe that anyone that wants to can run. And they can even run a marathon if they want to.

It's easy to find excuses and to put things off until tomorrow, next week or after payday. But if running is something you want to do and being more active, healthier and generally more awesome is something that you want to be, you're going to have to start some time.

So if you bought this book for yourself because you want to start running or someone else bought it for you because you keep saying how you're going to become a runner, then stop putting it off and start doing it. If, however, you got it in the office secret Santa or found it on a park bench – might I suggest a local charity shop?

Chapter 1

How it all began – How to start running

THERE are two words in the English language that fill me with dread and put me off exercise for a long time: gym induction. It was early 2008 and I had decided months earlier that I needed to start exercising. I weighed up the options and concluded that joining an expensive gym metres from my office was the perfect balance of being too handy and too expensive for me to even consider not going. The gym induction, however, was the first barrier to starting my new guilt-based training plan. It's like being the new kid at school, being paraded around the gym by an instructor and shown how all the various equipment works and, worse still, being made to use it while they look on assessing just how unfit you are.

Luckily when the day and time of my gym induction arrived, the person inducting me had something more urgent to be doing. She looked me up and down, my small build fooling her, and she said: "You look pretty fit. You know how all this stuff works don't you?" I then did something I'm not proud of. I lied like a teenage virgin who has been asked about their 'first time'. "Yeah, of course. I've been a gym goer for, like, years. Since I was ten. Probably earlier. I was born in a gym. Literally. I love these machines. I could use them standing on my head. Obviously I won't though, because of health and safety. I love the gym. I'd live in the gym if I could. I would just curl up at night on one of those squishy things...yeah the exercise mats, of course I know what they are, I was checking you do."

I hated the gym.

So I was cut loose on the gym equipment, free to use the pulley thing, the steppy thing, the pushy thing, the bike (I knew that one) and the running thing to my heart's content. Over the coming weeks I would realise that the weights were always occupied by grunting men or chatting women, the exercise bike was less comfy and less handy than the bike gathering dust in my own garage, and the cross trainer was a futile activity that had no perceivable use in the real world. The only machine I had any interest in was the treadmill. Unlike the cross trainer, the treadmill could have tangible benefits for me outside the four walls of the gym. If I could learn to run a mile on the treadmill I could, presumably, run a mile on the road and this might be useful in situations where I had to run away from someone or to the shop before it closed. Never again would I miss a bus or last orders because I'd be running there. This was where running started to seem like a good idea: in a gym in central London during my lunch break. There was only one problem: I was rubbish at running.

Apart from those annoying people who could run pretty much as soon as they could walk and who always looked forward to the annual school sports day with the excitement that most of us save for Christmas or a pint at the end of a long week, everyone sucks at running when they first start. I wasn't a natural runner. I skived off school on school sports days. I skived off PE and I couldn't run one lap of the running track without collapsing with a stitch. I also hated the sporty kids because, while me and my frizzy ginger hair and sparrow legs got laughed at, they were applauded. Most of the first 26 years of my life were spent avoiding exercise.

Joining the gym in 2008 was my second attempt at starting running. On my first attempt, shortly after finishing university, I had slowly worked my way up to the giddy heights of being able to run one kilometre without stopping before I decided that early retirement was the next logical step for my running career. So, when I came out of retirement in 2008 to give it another shot, the running world was not worried.

This is where I should have thought about reading up on running, perhaps gone to a running shop for some advice or maybe come clean about my athletic inability and asked the gym instructor some questions. But none of these things happened. The short story is that I tried to run too far, too fast, too soon in trainers that were too small and I got injured. The long story goes like this...

My early training plan consisted of running as far as I could at a number on the treadmill that didn't seem feeble in comparison to the person on the treadmill next to me, and then collapsing in a big heap. The next time I went to the gym I would try to run further. I've since read a lot about the science behind running and different training techniques, and the experts seem in agreement that this is not the best way to avoid injuring yourself.

I still have my notebook in which I recorded my early training. The highlight of my first month of gym membership was that I was able to run for five minutes non-stop. It seemed like a huge achievement for me at the time – and it was. But if I try something new, I want to be good at it straight away – which is why I usually give up after a few attempts. I wanted results. I wanted to see big numbers on the display of the treadmill rather than the kilometre and a half I was capable of in the early days. So after not very long I ignored conventional wisdom of 'building up gradually' to try running for as long as I could, and as hard as I could. I gave myself the target of running non-stop for ten minutes before the end of May and on 19th May I achieved my goal with much panting and a very painful stitch.

In June I gave myself the target of upping this to 15 minutes of non-stop running and just five days into the month I managed it. All was going well, perhaps too well, and disaster couldn't be far off. A week or so later I got a cold and sore throat, and with this came the perfect excuse to avoid the gym. I had heard all the stories of stupidly fit athletes who exercised with a cold and dropped down dead – I wasn't taking any chances. Staying on the sofa, watching *Hollyoaks* and eating Kit Kats seemed like far and away the best option.

After two weeks of skiving off the gym (it's so much easier when you don't have to forge a note from your mum) I was back and anticipating another PB. But no, my two-week break had put me back and I was struggling to get eight minutes on the clock. It took another month of trying to get back up to my previous record of 15 minutes running, but then I had a breakthrough: 20 minutes of non-stop running and a distance of 3.6km! I felt like an Olympian.

I've now run four marathons, the most recent one in three hours 56 minutes and in preparation for a marathon I will run 20 miles through the streets of London by myself. Did I think, three years ago that either of those things would ever happen? Probably not. But I did want them to be true. And here's the thing I learnt about myself: I'm a stubborn little git and stubbornness trumps over impatience. Stubbornness is what got me from zero to 3.6km.

Stubbornness is what gets me through 20 lonely, painful miles. It was stubbornness that made me persevere with the gym, even though it seemed to dislike me as much as I hated it and even though there was somewhere more interesting that I could be, like at home on the sofa, at the cinema with friends or pretty much anywhere but on the treadmill. But this time I wouldn't quit.

What I wish I had known then

Getting started

You don't need to be a member of a gym, have fancy kit or join a club to start running, you just need a bit of space and a bit of motivation. Starting running in the gym was a security blanket for me. I knew I could get off the treadmill and stop at any time. But this is true when you run outdoors too – you can stop and walk any time you like. It's ok to walk. It's good to walk. Beginners' training plans start with 'run/walk' combinations of running for a few minutes then walking for a few minutes. Gradually the running bits will get longer and the walking bits shorter until you're running the whole way. Even after that, you may still find yourself having to stop and walk during training runs or even during races – but walk with your head held high. There's no shame in walking. Walk like you mean it.

In races, walking often draws shouts of encouragement to start running again from spectators. This can be helpful and motivating but it can also be annoying when you feel spent and would gladly lie down in the street and not get up if 1,000 people behind you weren't about to stamp on your head the moment you did. As a spectator I've shouted my tonsils raw calling out "come on, you can do it" at marathon runners. One of the best examples of walking with your head held high was a man I saw dressed as a fairy at mile 24 of the London Marathon, walking with a strut and a wiggle that would put Kate Moss to shame.

In short, starting running is very simple – just get out there and run and don't expect too much of yourself too soon. Take it easy, find a training plan that starts at the level that you're at now and that looks achievable as it progresses (but that pushes you). The starting is the easy part, it's the carrying on that's the tough part as I was about to discover.

Get your body moving.
Go outside to a local park or a quiet street and run and walk for about 20 minutes. Get your legs moving – not because you're on your way somewhere – but for the fun of it. It doesn't matter how much of the 20 minutes you spend running or walking, you're getting to know how far you can move in that time, how fit you are and where in your local area is a good place for you to become a runner. This is your starting point.

Make time to run
Look at your diary or calendar and set aside three half-hour slots a week for the next couple of weeks. This is when you are going to run. It might be in the morning, after work or on the weekends. Try to space them out throughout the week to give your body time to recover from each session, but make that commitment to making time to run.

Find a training plan
In the Resources section of this book you will find a list of places to go to find a training plan that is right for you. Whether your goal is just to start running and work up to running non-stop for half an hour, or whether you want to leap straight in and train for a marathon, there's a training plan out there that has you covered. It might not feel like it right now, but it's common

for new runners to do too much too soon. Sticking to a training plan will help you train safely and avoid injury.

Get some running shoes

We'll cover the essential kit you need, as well as the kit you don't, in the next chapter. But for now, look up your local running store and pay them a visit. They'll be able to advise you on the right sort of trainers for you. Buying running shoes isn't about which are the nicest colour or go best with your jogging bottoms, a good running shop will look at your 'gait' (the way your feet land when you run) and advise you on the shoes that are best for you to help you avoid getting injured.

Chapter 2

If the shoe fits – Getting kitted out

"WHAT size shoe do you take?" It was an easy enough question and it concerned my own feet – feet that had belonged to me for 26 years and that, for the past ten years at least, hadn't changed shape or size. But apparently I had answered incorrectly. "No, there's no way you're a size four. You're a five and a half at least." This was information that I couldn't get my head round. It was like being told I had been spelling my name wrong for the whole of my adult life.

I had known since I started running that I needed proper running shoes but I was reluctant to pay for a pair of special trainers for something I may yet give up on. Though I, like a lot of people, love getting new shoes – a pair of running shoes comes with a commitment. I have a sewing machine and a climbing harness sat in the bottom of the wardrobe from previous new hobbies that I soon got bored of or that became too complicated to keep up. I didn't need to spend £80 on a pair of trainers only to do the same.

But I'd read that going to a running shop to get properly fitted with the right sort of shoes could save me a lot of pain and possible injury. And I was all about avoiding pain. I imagined it would feel rather like when you were a child and you would go to get your feet measured for your new school shoes. Why doesn't that happen once you reach adulthood? I would have less pairs of shoes that I wore once and then gave up on because

I couldn't tolerate the pain if Topshop brought in a shoe fitter. But instead of being happy when the woman assessing the size of my feet announced I needed a bigger size, on this occasion I was mortified.

For the first few months I had been running in a pair of old trainers that I'd had for about five years but that were still box fresh and dazzling white. It's fair to say they hadn't done many miles. They were about £20 in the sale and were more 'fashion trainers' than being intended for taking part in any actual sport, but that just about summed up the old me. I was ready to welcome in the new me and that involved some ugly, functional training shoes!

I went to a running shop where they assess your 'gait', or how your feet land when you run, and suggest a shoe based on this. This involves being filmed running on a treadmill (thankfully all knee down stuff, totally PG-rated footage) and having the film slowed down to show you how your foot hits the floor. My feet were landing at some strange angle that made me worry my legs were about to snap in half at any moment. The woman in the shop handed me the ugliest pair of trainers I had ever seen and told me to hop back on the treadmill. She filmed me again then played back the footage of me running in the ugly shoes – luckily the camera didn't capture my unimpressed face. My feet no longer looked like they were trying to work themselves free of my legs. I was sold. I bounced out the shop clutching my ugly trainers and feeling like a real runner. No longer would I be embarrassed by my feet at the gym. I had the gear now – but sadly, still no idea about many things when it came to running.

After two months plodding away on the treadmill at the gym I was feeling quite confident. If at 12noon sharp I picked up my bag and headed out the office before my mind was aware of where I was going, I could be on the treadmill picking up the pace before my legs had chance to object. I learnt a few tricks too like telling myself that if it wasn't going well after two minutes, I could give up. "Just two minutes more and then you can stop" I would tell myself. I usually didn't stop though. Using these motivational techniques, that I like to call 'lying to yourself', I could now trick my legs into running for half an hour non-stop and cover around 4.5km on the treadmill. But I still didn't feel like a 'real' runner yet.

The weather was getting nicer and I had seen people running outside, sun on their faces, wind in their hair, dog poo on their trainers. They were the 'real' runners. Running outside was new, scary territory, but I wanted to be a real runner and real runners do it outside. So one Saturday morning, kitted out with my new running shoes, I was ready to pound the pavements of South West London.

Only nobody told me that running on the road is different to running on a treadmill. My first attempt at running outdoors felt like the sort of running you do in a dream where you're being chased, only someone has knocked the gravity dial up a few notches and you struggle to get away from your assailant. My chest felt like it was being gradually pulled towards the ground and I managed what can only be termed as a 'shuffle' around the park before limping home having completed just 2.5km. It was half of what I could do in the gym and I felt dejected. For the next week I didn't run a single step. My shoes sat unused by the door while I sat on the sofa and sulked. The sofa was my friend, it had never let me down and never made me feel useless.

The ugly trainers stared at me every time I left the flat without them. They pleaded for another shot before they were forced to join the sewing machine and climbing harness in the wardrobe of forgotten hobbies. I thought about it and concluded that when running on the treadmill I was used to watching the minutes and kilometres tick away. This gave me something to focus on, to gauge how far I had gone and allowed me to push myself a bit further each time. When I had run on the road I had no idea how long or how far I'd been going and I gave in to discomfort earlier than I would have on the treadmill. I needed a new plan and a new weapon in my arsenal. So I headed to the shops and bought the cheapest sports watch I could find. It was £10, designed for children and instead of a buckle or clasp it fastened with Velcro. It was hardly the flashiest bit of kit going. I knew that I could run for 30 minutes non-stop in the gym so I just needed a stopwatch to reassure me and keep me going.

I headed out the door now kitted out with ugly shoes and a children's sports watch. I ignored the people around me, I ignored the voice in my head telling me to stop and go home to eat chocolate biscuits, I just kept looking at the few metres ahead of me and the number on my watch with the aim of doing 20 minutes on the tarmac. I negotiated all sorts of obstacles that, while walking, don't seem a problem: gravel; curbs; grass; pigeons; but each of these challenges broke up my stride, made me slow or stop and made it difficult to keep going. Inclines that I had never noticed before seemed to appear round every corner to steal what breath I had left. But, very slowly, 20 minutes ticked by and I had managed to run two miles outside without stopping. Although I was feeling more exhausted at the end of it than I would have after 30 minutes on the treadmill, I felt ok enough to know I could tag on an extra few minutes to my next al fresco run.

There was no fancy gadgetry – no heart rate monitor, no mileage tracking, no GPS – on my watch, just a stopwatch, but it helped me become a real runner who did it outside. There was no stopping me now! Or at least, that's what I thought.

What I wish I had known then
What do you need to run?
The great thing about running is that you need very little in the way of kit. This is just one of the reasons I'm a runner and not likely to become a tobogganist or round-the-world yachts person. But there are a few things that I've found that make running easier or more enjoyable and a couple of things that are essential.

ESSENTIALS
Shoes
Go along to your local running shop and talk to them about what sort of shoes might be right for you. Maybe get your gait assessed, but at the very least, get a pair that are the right size. I now wear a pair of size six running shoes instead of the size four I blindly started out in and, so far, I've escaped any serious injury. It's recommended that you replace your running shoes every 500 miles. While that may seem quite a long way off, if

you're starting out in a pair of trainers you've had for years, their best days may already be behind them.

Barefoot running enthusiasts would argue that shoes aren't necessary at all. It is possible to run without shoes. I ran five miles barefoot on a beach once and ran a half-marathon in Bangkok with a man who wore only socks. This isn't a lifestyle choice everyone wants to make, but if you want to give it a go you should seek specialist advice first.

One cold winter day I went out for a run wearing a hoodie and two pairs of gloves, that's how cold I was. The next day I put on even more layers and went out on my bike only to be shamed by a barefoot runner (he was wearing 'minimal shoes' – basically socks with a thin rubber sole). I like to think that I'm not a wimp, but when it comes to my feet I would rather drink the limescaley contents of my hot water bottle than take one step on a frozen path going barefoot. Even if I did go shoeless, I think I would be a fair-weather barefooter.

Sports bra

If I was stranded on a desert island and could take one item with me, it would be a good sports bra. It's the one and only item I think I'd need in order to run. Shoes wouldn't be much use on sand, it gets inside them and irritates your feet, but I couldn't run without a sports bra. For women runners, a sports bra is, in my opinion, the most essential piece of kit.

They come in different levels of effectiveness depending on the type of sport you intend to wear them for because sports like cycling, for example, involve much less bounce than running. You're looking for sports bras that say things like 'extra high impact' on them or are intended specifically for running. When you try one on, jump up and down in the changing room for a little while to test it out.

BENEFICIAL
Sports clothing

The main thing to worry about when dressing for your run is that you're comfortable and you'll find out what's still comfortable for you after a few miles of running largely through trial and error. There are certain fabrics that are designed to make your run more comfortable by allowing sweat to evaporate. Most sports clothing will claim to use 'wicking technology'. This generally means it's some sort of man-made fabric designed to cope with sweat.

In the summer this sort of fabric allows sweat to evaporate and cool you down, and likewise, in the winter it allows sweat to escape so that you don't get cold. Cotton fabrics absorb sweat and therefore don't help much in either situation so a short sleeved sports top in summer and a long-sleeved 'base layer' sports top for winter is a good investment. They should fit close to your body so that they can get sweaty but don't need to be tight. On cold days you might want to add a t-shirt over the top of your 'wicking' base top and you can use any old t-shirt for this.

Stopwatch

As you've seen above, a watch with a simple stopwatch function can help. If you're starting with a run/walk schedule it will help you measure your run and walk sections accurately and time the total amount of time you've been running so you can track your progress. These can be found for around £10.

Running backpack

Squeezing runs into your weekly routine can be a tricky business. A small backpack that fits you properly will enable you to run home from work or to a friend's house while carrying your valuables and a change of clothes. You can buy backpacks that have been specially designed for running and they come in different sizes, so you might need to try a few to find one that fits you best. A strap that fits around the waist and one that fastens across the chest will help to keep it from bouncing around and rubbing as you run, and will help take some of the weight off your shoulders.

ADVERSE WEATHER
Cap

The humble cap is a useful and versatile piece of kit. It's much more practical than sunglasses for keeping the sun out of the eyes while running and has proved essential on many a sunny long run. But far from just being a piece of summer headwear, the cap is an ever-present in my kit bag. When it rains the seasoned runner isn't deterred, and with the aid of a cap (preferably with plastic in the peak instead of cardboard which can get soggy) they can carry on clocking up the miles without rain getting in their eyes.

Waterproofs
Waterproof jackets can vary in how much they cost and how effective they are. There are two problems they need to overcome – keeping the rain out and letting sweat escape. In summer rain can be a welcome relief to cool you off, but the thought of heading out the door when it's chucking it down can be made more appealing by knowing your jacket will keep you reasonably dry.

Winter kit
There are several calendar-related rules in the fashion world such as "you can't wear white trousers after 1st September" or "you have to wear that dodgy Christmas jumper your Gran knitted you until after Boxing Day". The clocks going back officially marks the start of the winter kit season and during the winter months your kit needs to do two things: make sure you stay warm, and make sure you're visible to cars so you don't get run over. So when choosing winter kit, the brighter the better is a good rule to follow.

Hi-visibility top or jacket
Granted, they don't come in the most flattering of colours, but make sure you're seen by other road users. It's much more flattering than being run over. Choosing one with a spot of waterproofing and windproofing will also help to keep you dry and toasty.

Gloves
There are two types of weather in winter: one-pair-of-gloves days and two-pairs-of-gloves days. I have a pair of running gloves as my 'base layer' but when it gets super frosty I add my 'reserve gloves' a bog-standard £1.99 pair of gloves on

top. Both come in handy for wiping your nose on. Come on, we all do it!

Old t-shirts

Cotton race t-shirts are mostly too big and unsuitable for running in during the summer, but winter is when they come in handy. Wear them above your base layer for a bit of warmth. And they're usually long enough to cover your bum if you're a newcomer to wearing lycra in public. Which brings me on to...

Running tights

Gentlemen, don't be shy – we understand that it's cold. Yes, the words 'tights' and 'leggings' will put you off a bit but there's no reason to be a hero when it's cold by suffering in bare legs. If you're shy, maybe ease yourself in with a pair of shorts over the top.

NICE TO HAVE
Gadgetry (heart rate monitors and GPS watches)

The watch I now use has GPS tracking and can do a lot of things that will make me faster: there's the 'virtual training partner', structured workouts, and a heart rate monitor – all of which I never use. I hate to think of my watch getting frustrated every time I put it on just to measure the same old routes, but my brain doesn't seem to be complaining about watching the same old TV just yet.

However, my GPS watch has made running a lot simpler (maybe because I don't exploit its functionality to the full). I put on my kit and my watch and then just run in whatever direction I fancy, knowing that when I look down at my wrist I'll know how far I've gone and how fast I got there. Gone are the days of tirelessly clicking on a Google map to see how many miles a lap of the park is or trying to remember if I went left or right at that junction. For a lazy runner like me, something to measure how far you went is a must. I think my little green mileage machine has also helped my running. The key to running further is running slower, so by telling me my speed my watch has taught me to slow down on long runs.

If you have a smartphone there are a lot of GPS running apps available (examples in the Resources section) that will measure your route as you run and provide time, distance and speed information. That's the most you'll need to know for a good while.

What to do now

Think about the kit that you've been running in. Is there anything listed above that would help you?

If you haven't already, have a look at the shoes you're running in. Are they fit for the job? Do they fit properly with a bit of space at the end of the toes for your feet to move forward as you run? How do the soles look? Are the worn down in places? Uneven wear can be a sign that your feet are landing awkwardly. Do you need to pay a visit to a running shop?

If you've so far only run on the treadmill, venture outside for a run. Take it steady. Without the treadmill to pace you you're likely to go off too fast so slow down, relax and enjoy it. And watch out for the dog poo.

Chapter 3

800 metres of shame – What's stopping you running?

SOMEBODY had to run the 800m race. Faces stared blankly back at our form tutor and nobody put their hand up. The organisation of year nine school sports day was almost done, the fast runners had filled up the 100m and 200m spots, the taller among the class had signed-up for the high jump and long jump, and the sporty kids had volunteered to do whatever else was needed. Each person was allowed to compete in a maximum of three events and there was just one event not filled. It was the 800m or two laps of the running track that had been marked out in the grass in white paint for the summer months.

I put my hand up "Ok, I'll do it. But I'll come last." A collective sigh went round among those who, like me, were not suited to more than a short dash for the school bus. Two laps of the field couldn't go that badly could it? It could.

Come last in the 100m and people barely even notice. Everyone is focussed on the winner leaving those in sixth, seventh and eighth to sneak over the line while nobody is looking. Not so with the 800m. The gun went off and we all started running.

By the time the leaders finished their first lap, I was barely 300m around mine. By the time I got to 600m I was having to walk and the winner had finished. All eyes were on me as

I tried to run round the final bend but was forced to walk the remaining 200m by myself. I hated sports day and the next year I would be 'absent' because I hated running and would avoid it at all costs for the next 15 years. But it hadn't always been that way.

Kelly Wilkinson was the fastest girl in my primary school. This had long been established through years of lunchtime playground contests. She beat all the other girls and some of the boys too. We would all line up with one hand on a wall waiting for our official starter to shout go before all running full pelt to the other side of the playground to see who would touch the opposite wall first and claim victory. The winners and losers were the same each race, but that didn't keep us from lining up time after time. We didn't just run to compete in these sprints, we ran away from each other playing tag and towards each other for British Bulldog. Whatever the game, we were running.

When the annual school sports day came around we lined up on the school field in our class groups. The obstacle race, beanbag on head race, the skipping race were all very well but, like the Olympics, the 100m sprint was very much the blue riband event. It was a hot summer's day and my mum had brought my teenage brother (who is nine years older than me) along with one of his friends and our dog to watch. The four of them did a Mexican wave as they sat in the shade on the far side of the playing field. I lined up for my heat and when the teacher shouted "go" I ran as quickly as my legs would carry me. It was the sort of running you do as a child where you're constantly on the verge of falling forward to the ground. Eventually I broke the tape – I was the winner of my heat and I was ecstatic.

I was through to the final where I lined up against Kelly Wilkinson. I had been watching her in her heat and in various playground races, and I'd noticed that she slowed down towards the end of the race. My ten-year-old mind was of the opinion that, if I could just keep running fast all the way to the line I might just be able to catch her. We were under starter's orders: ready, set, go! Kelly ran, I ran, everyone watched as we headed for the finish line. Kelly was first to cross it. I followed in third place.

In a year's time I would be moving up to senior school and everything would change. The playground was no longer a place where we played tag or British Bulldog or raced each other. They were children's games. Where once running was fun and easy, something we did without even thinking about it, running would become, for me, something that hurt, something that made me look stupid and something that should be avoided. I hung up my plimsolls and I forgot how to run. More importantly I forgot how to enjoy running.

What I wish I had known then
What's stopping you?
Putting off starting things is a skill. It takes years of practice and I've mastered all seven levels of procrastination. When it comes to starting running, I'll bet that most people are like me – it's not so much the laziness that is keeping you from starting but fear. I was scared of running. Not in the same way that people are scared of spiders or snakes, I wasn't scared that my trainers were going to leap out from under the sofa and stamp on my big toe – but I was scared all the same. It was a fear of many things: fear of what people would think, fear of what I would look like, fear of it hurting or of not being very good at it. But I told myself that I was a grown-up who can sleep in the dark, get rid of spiders she finds in the bath and laugh in the face of clowns, and gradually I found that there really was nothing to be scared of when it came to running too. Let me explain.

What will I look like?
Hair pulled back, no make-up on, sweat dripping off your chin – you might think that running is you looking at your worst, but I disagree. There's a shelf in my mum's house with four pictures on. Three are wedding pictures of my sister and two brothers on their wedding days and they look nice. The fourth has a picture of me in it. I have sweat all over my face, snot on my t-shirt and a cap covering messy hair. In reality, I don't look the best I ever have and it's definitely not how I'd choose to look for things like going on a date, going to court or picking up my OBE. But at the same time I look pretty awesome. I'm halfway round my first marathon and I'm smiling.

Running may not make you look too pretty, not in the way that conforms to conventional representations of how 'pretty' is presented to us in magazines and on TV. But looking awesome is different to looking pretty. There are some people out there who only run at the gym or after dark through fear of being seen running and sweating by people who aren't. Or worse, there are people who run with full make-up on and perfect hair without it ever getting messed up. I once saw a woman running with her hair in a beehive and full make-up, neither of which were going anywhere because there was no sweat and no effort and I felt sorry for her.

If you're bothered how you look when you're running, you're going to hold something back. Sweat is the sign of a good run. The more you sweat, the more impressed you should be with your reflection. Think of it less as sweat and more as awesome juice.

So if you're worried about what you look like when you run, next time you get home from running, go stand in front of the mirror and if you've worked hard and sweated hard, no matter what shape or size you are, repeat after me: "This is what awesome looks like."

What will people think?

This may come as a surprise to you be but the world on the whole doesn't really care about you. And that, in this instance, is a good thing. It's not that you've done anything wrong or that you're not special, it's just that most people are self absorbed and concerned mainly with themselves. They don't notice you running down the street or on the treadmill next to them at the gym. That's why runners wear neon colours – not just to be seen in the dark but to be seen at all and not get run over.

When it comes to people who know you and are supposed to care about you, what they think could be one of two things: "good on you – keep at it" or "pah, you'll not last five minutes". Now those that are thinking the latter are known by the technical term 'haters'. In terms of starting running, you have three options available to you to deal with haters:

1 Don't even bother starting running – prove them right.
2 Start, but give up after a week or two – prove them right.
3 Start running, enjoy it and don't care what anyone says.

I started running twice before I became a runner. By this I mean that I tried running for a couple of weeks and gave up again. On the third time I stuck with it, started enjoying it and became a runner. There's no badge or initiation ceremony for becoming a runner – there was just a point, I don't exactly know when, at which running became part of my everyday life and something that is part of my identity. If I was to go on a TV quiz show and was asked to introduce myself I would say: "Hi, I'm Laura. I live in London, I like curry, I don't like liquorice or people who say 'whilst' instead of 'while' and I'm a runner." So that's another good reason to ignore haters and start running – so you'll have something to say in awkward meet and greet situations.

I won't be very good at it

This is true, you won't be very good at it. Not at first. You won't be good at most things the first time you try them. Getting better at running isn't just a case of getting fitter – there's stuff you have to learn too like how to pace yourself, breathing, when is best for you to run and what post-run rewards work best to motivate you. Most of this stuff you'll work out for yourself through practice as you go along. As you run more you'll work out what works best for you. And as you get fitter it will feel easier, and you'll get better at it. But on day one you will suck big time and you won't be able to ever imagine a day when running will be effortless or fun, and you will want to give up. But it's important that you don't.

There are probably other things you've done in your life that you, at first, thought were impossible. When I was learning to drive a car I came home after one lesson and thought I may as well give up. It was impossible. I'd had 15 hours of lessons and it just didn't seem to be working for me. I sensed even my driving instructor was giving up on me and that I was wasting money on lessons. A couple of lessons later something clicked and I could drive a car, and eventually (after two tries) I passed my driving test. Running was a similar process, I'm impatient and I wanted to see results straight away. The first time I went on the treadmill in the gym I ran for ten minutes covering 1.14km and that involved walking parts of it. It was slow progress but you know how that story ends.

It takes more courage to head out for your second ever run than it does to line up for the start of a marathon. At the start of your second run you know how rubbish you are at it, you know it won't be a pleasant experience and you're willing to do it anyway – even though there's nobody giving you a medal at the end. So I salute you. This is one of the things that keeps me running – the thought of having to go back to square one and start all over again is enough to keep me going.

It will hurt

If you're reading this the chances are that you've tried to run at least once already, so I can't lie to you and pretend it's not going to hurt. There's a sort of discomfort that running can inflict on the body where your limbs feel like lead, your lungs burn and your gums ache. You'll find all sorts of inspirational quotes such as "pain is inevitable, suffering is optional" or "pain is weakness leaving the body", but for me these have never worked, though I'm sure they make some people feel better for having on their t-shirt.

What I want to tell you is that fear of being uncomfortable or running hurting will probably never go away. While running for a couple of miles will get easier the more you do it, the fear of pain won't go away. I still have it, most people probably experience it. You'll feel your run is making you suffer if you are pushing beyond your boundaries and in the early days you'll be doing this a lot. At first pushing yourself might be trying to run a mile without stopping, in time it could be trying to get a five kilometre PB or finishing a marathon. As long as you keep pushing yourself and challenging yourself you'll be experiencing a certain amount of discomfort. But you will probably find that the sense of achievement on reaching your goals outweighs it and lasts a lot longer than those aching muscles do.

I fear track sessions because I know they hurt. Not only while I do it but the next day too. I fear the marathon because I know how much it hurts to hit the wall. I fear trying for a PB because I know that running to my limit hurts and getting three quarters of the way through a race only to see your goal slipping away hurts even more. But I also fear being ordinary, I fear regrets of the things I didn't do, I fear not trying and I fear asking "what if?" Fear of getting wet, getting cold or overheating all come into this category too – but with the right kit you can get around these problems.

Let me be clear though – if ever running is painful you should stop straight away and seek medical advice.

Running can makes you feel invincible and like you can achieve anything you set your mind to. There's lots of things that I was scared to do besides running. Things I really wanted to do but I thought were beyond me. But then I ran a marathon and that changed the way I looked at the world in terms of what was possible and what was not.

I'm too old/fat/lazy to be a runner

You might think you're too old to run, or too fat to run – I can tell you for a fact that you're not.

Aged 50, Mike Hare, the self-titled "Incredible Shrinking Man", weighed 28 stone. After he was involved in a car crash Mike decided to get fit and took up running. Mike lost 15 stone, and as a challenge, just six months after starting running he completed his first half-marathon – the Great North Run. Five months after having major surgery to remove huge flaps of loose skin left over from all the weight he had lost, and now aged 54, he completed the London Marathon. He went on to complete the Edinburgh Marathon, a second Great North Run, the Great Eastern Run, and the Athens Classic Marathon. Still think you're too fat?

Rosie Swale-Pope picked up a running magazine in a doctor's waiting room and decided to take up running. On her 57th birthday, following the death of her husband, Rosie set off from her home in Wales to run around the world. Her 19,900-mile unsupported journey took her 1,789 days to complete. Fauja Singh, from East London, took up running marathons after being inspired by watching the London Marathon- he was 89 at the time. Fauja completed eight marathons in London, Toronto and New York before retiring from the distance aged

101. He now concentrates on shorter distance races. Still think you're too old to run?

What to do now

What is it that's stopping you from starting running? Be honest. What is it that you're scared of? Write it down.

"I'm scared to start running because..."

Now write down in big letters:

"But I won't let this stop me becoming a runner."

The only way to tackle your fears is to get out there and go for a run. So what are you waiting for? Off you go.

Chapter 4

Getting competitive –
The race

SEVERAL hundred years ago my ancestors arrived in the UK from continental Europe. They pitched up their tents, or whatever they lived in back then, in the east of the country and they set about digging in the swampy ground. This is the reason why I'm not very good at running up hills. My ancestors dug the dykes that drained The Fens and reclaimed the area we now know as East Anglia from the sea. Generation after generation of Fountains have lived on the flattest ground around and over time whatever bit of muscle it is that allows people to get up (and down) a hill quickly without injury got smaller. I've genetically evolved to live on the flat. That's my unsubstantiated theory at least.

When it came to signing up for my first race, I forgot all about my genetic predisposition to flat ground. My quest to be a 'real runner' was going well. I was able to run outside for 20 minutes and I had dog pooh on my trainers to prove it. I was excited by the fact that I could now run five kilometres on a treadmill without stopping, but frustrated that I was still not able to complete the same distance out on the street in the real world. 'Real runners' were running races, throwing cups of water over themselves and getting medals for their efforts. So I decided that's what I needed to do: I needed to sign up for a 10km race. I signed up for the Wimbledon 10k, a small race of around 500 runners that started close to my flat. It was 14 weeks away giving me plenty of time to add a little bit each week to the distance I could run and build up slowly. The race would give me a little extra push to keep training and a goal to focus on. It sounded ideal. There was just one problem: it involved a massive hill.

My equally lazy flatmate Rostam decided to join me in my goal of completing the Wimbledon 10k. Apart from the odd game of football on a Sunday afternoon, Rostam didn't run and being from the same home town, he was as unaccustomed as I was to running. We were both much better suited to sitting at home on the sofa, however I would rather watch *EastEnders* while he, rather ironically I thought, wanted to stare at sport. Somewhere between deciding to do the race and handing over our entry fee, a wager had been made: the winner got exclusive rights to the remote control for a month. This just got serious.

We trained separately, him in his gym and me in mine, plus a few miles on the road. We talked about our training and how on earth we were going to get up the hill. Our flat was at the base of the hill so every time I went out to the door it was there staring at me and intimidating me. Wimbledon Common is a great place to run – there's always a new path to go down and get lost along. The Common is at the top of the hill, so to go running there I would always walk up the hill and then start my run once I got to the top. I knew exactly how big it was and how out of breath it made me just walking up it. My local pub was at the top of the hill too and once in the depths of winter when Rostam and I had spent the afternoon there we slid down the hill in the snow with an estate agent's sign as a makeshift sledge, so we had a good idea how steep it was too. There was no way I could run up it in the race. There was only one way to deal with the hill: I would have to run up it in training.

I set off to run two miles. First I would run one mile on the flat road at the bottom of the hill then, once I was warmed up, like Kate Bush I'd be running up that hill. I had hoped that I'd discover that it wasn't so bad after all. That it would be hard but ok and I would get to the top without stopping. But my hopes were in vain. Instead, I had to stop running less than half way up. I couldn't get started again and walked home with my confidence dented more than ever before. The hill was halfway round the 10k route, so even if I was able to run 10k, the hill might stop me from even finishing the first five kilometres of the race. It didn't look good.

After a few more weeks of training, it was time to stop living in fear and give it another go. I set out to conquer the hill or at least conquer my fear of it. I changed my midweek two-mile route to include the hill and set off. What starts off as a gradual slope soon becomes steep and at this point the hill threw me an opt-out: a woman with a suitcase stopped me to ask me directions to a road I had never heard of. I could have stopped and chatted – caught my breath and rested my legs for a minute, but I didn't. Instead I shouted "sorry, I can't help you" over my shoulder and plodded onwards.

I slowed down, I was going almost as slow as a quick walk and expected pensioners to overtake me at any moment, but I carried on putting one foot in front of the other and focussing a couple of metres in front of me. Eventually I made it all the way to the top without stopping, which was a huge achievement for me. Then came the flat ground. I wanted to know that my breathing and legs would return to their normal level of tiredness immediately – but they didn't. I had stopped going uphill but my legs were still complaining and my breathing was all over the place. But I carried on and after about half a mile on the flat I felt a bit better. I returned home, two-mile run complete and the hill conquered. I was ready!

A few days later my race number arrived for the Wimbledon 10k, I was number 54 – the low number indicative of the small field and how keen I had been in signing up for the race 14 weeks in advance. It was an exciting moment, I felt like a 'real runner'. On the reverse of the number, as on nearly all race numbers, was a form to fill in with your medical details and next of kin 'in case of emergency'. This was not reassuring.

Rostam, who had been training exclusively on the treadmill, decided to join me on an outdoors run just two weeks before the race. I knew he had put in less training than me but he had done a couple of big-ish runs (a 5k and a 6k) on the treadmill at his gym. This was worrying in terms of the little competition we had going about the remote control and to see which of us would make it over the finish line first. It took me a long time to get up to a five kilometre distance even on the treadmill and if he was able to do this after a shorter period of time, he might be able to beat me. It wasn't so much the losing that bothered me as it was the idea that something that had taken me six months to accomplish slogging it out at the gym and on the road could be achieved by someone else in just a few weeks. Was I really that bad at running?

We headed out with the intention of running five miles, but neither of us had ever run this far before. It was unknown territory. The first mile went faster than I had wanted and my attempts to slow us down didn't work. I started to get worried that Rostam would hold out for the whole five miles and have enough in the tank to beat me back to the front door. As we approached two and a half miles, Rostam's breathing was getting a bit louder. I may still have a chance, I thought. The chit-chat between us became less but we were both still capable of exchanging a few words.

As we approached three miles I explained where the route would take us and he asked how long we had been going. A check of the watch said 30 minutes of pounding the pavement had passed. Five minutes later he gave in and took a short cut back to the flat, walking most of the way. I was disappointed for him that he had to cut his run short, but I was elated that my training hadn't been in vain. I knew I'd done more training for this than Rostam had and it had paid off. The competition between us had put undue pressure on us both. With that now settled by way of our five-mile run, we could both relax and focus on the race. The only competition we had now was ourselves...and that massive hill.

The day of the race came and Rostam and I were joined by our friend Jon (a seasoned runner who at 50 would finish the race in 45 minutes) to walk down to the start. In my nervous excitement and haste to get out the door, I forgot my chip timing tag that had been posted out with my race number and should have been fastened round my ankle to give an accurate finish time. But I had my trusty stopwatch so that would have to do. After a few trips to the Portaloos we lined up at the start on a rugby pitch and waited for the gun, then we were off. The nervous chit-chat between runners waiting to get going died at the gun and the first few hundred metres of the race were deadly quiet. As we headed off the rugby field and onto a residential street the only sound to be heard was of hundreds of feet touching down on the tarmac. Rostam and I lost sight of each other in the pack during the first couple of hundred metres – parting with a shout of "good luck – see you at the finish". We took a couple of turns and were now running on the pavement of a usually busy street that, at 9am on a Sunday, was not too busy. The occasional passer-by would shout out words of encouragement as we passed, 500 runners shuffling along en mass. By the time we reached the hill at just under half way I was feeling pretty good. But I knew what was to come.

As we hit the base I slowed down, pumped my arms and focussed a few metres in front of me. People around me had started to walk but I was determined not to give in to the hill, so I carried on. I was overtaking other runners, this was completely unexpected. Although I felt awful, passing people felt great. A couple of hundred metres and I was at the top, the hill was over. The roads weren't closed to traffic and as I got to the top of the hill a marshal put up her arm to signal us runners to stop to allow cars to pass. It was a welcome ten-second break that allowed me to get my breath back. We carried on through Wimbledon Village past people sat in cafes having their breakfast and staring out at us. I would much rather have been the other side of the window at that moment tucking into some poached eggs on toast and reading the papers. But there was a weird sense of achievement that I wasn't; that I had got up early, eaten a bagel, a banana and set off to run a race and to push myself.

The last kilometre seemed to last forever. I was running hard, desperate to finish in under an hour. The route turned off the main road and up a slight incline towards the rugby field where we had started. It seemed much further than it had on the way out but finally the tarmac gave way to grass and I was on the home straight. I pushed with everything I had left and crossed the finish line in 57 minutes 17 seconds. I was tired, sweaty and everything ached but I loved it. I'd finished my first race. Six minutes later Rostam crossed the line and we proudly wore our medals down to a local pub.

What I wish I had known then
Goal setting

Before you can start doing anything, you need to know what your goals are. Whether you've admitted them out loud or not, you already have an idea of where you want to get to with your running. Turning that idea into a goal, or several smaller goals will help you focus and improve.

When I first started running I had two vague ideas in my mind. First was the romantic notion I had of running down a beach, care-free and effortlessly. I had seen people in films or on TV running down beaches, usually in America and usually looking very perfect and not sweating. I wanted some of that because to me that looked like true escapism. The running looked free and easy – a million miles away from the huffing and puffing I was doing on a treadmill with a stitch. It was the idea of enjoying running and doing it for fun that I was trying to get to. And the beach thing too.

In 2011 I spent Christmas Day in Australia and as the sun started to go down, I put on my sports bra and headed out to run barefoot down the beach for about five miles. It was free and easy, I enjoyed it and I'd made it to the place I wanted to. In truth I had enjoyed running for a long time already and had some runs that felt free and effortless. I just hadn't been doing it on a beach.

The second goal I had was to run a marathon. It was a goal that seemed even further away from where I was, struggling to run a mile without stopping, than running free and easy seemed. But I had watched the London Marathon as a child as I looked out for my uncle who ran it year after year. I had stood on the sidelines as an adult and seen all the people go past and they didn't look that different from me. They weren't super-human, they weren't all built like athletes, they were just ordinary people who had decided they wanted to run 26.2 miles and had put in enough time and effort to get themselves there.

Two years after tentatively starting out on the treadmill, able to run a maximum of five minutes without stopping I ran my first marathon in Brighton. There were times that I thought I wouldn't do it. After my first ever race, the idea of running an extra 20 miles on top of the distance I had just run sounded ludicrous. But there was a moment at the Brighton Marathon, not at the finish line but with about four miles to go, that someone in the crowd shouted: "Come on Laura. You can do it." And I said out loud: "Yes, I can do this." I knew that I was going to finish and that I was going to make my goal of running all the way. Neither of these things need to be your goal. But you should think about what your goal might be. And even if you do want to run a marathon, you'll probably need a few intermediate goals to get you there.

Example goals
* Run a mile without stopping.
* Run a 5k race.
* Run three times a week for a month.
* Run for half an hour.
To get you to your goal you'll need a training plan. There are a few places to go to find a training plan suitable for you and you'll find a couple listed in the Resources section at the back of this book.

Measuring progress
One of the most useful training tools you'll find is a pen and a piece of paper. Whether you run outside or on a treadmill after each run write down how long you ran for, what distance you covered and how you felt. Keep doing that and over time you'll be able to see yourself improving. You may have run for ten minutes each time for the first few weeks, but have you felt less exhausted each time you ran? You may have been able to run for slightly longer each time or you may have taken less walking breaks.

Knowing where you've come from and seeing in black and white that you're getting better is a huge confidence booster. Use a notebook, record it in your diary, on your computer or log it in an online training diary (there are a few of these listed in the Resources section).

Decide what your ultimate goal is, and write it down and then break it down into steps. What do you need to do to reach your goal? Write down any intermediate goals to help you get there too.

Chapter 5

Going further: The half-marathon

THE start of one race is pretty much the same as the start of any other. A long queue for the Portaloos, the smell of Deep Heat in the air, motivational music pumping over a tannoy with an unintelligible announcer shouting instructions, at runners who stand around looking nervous and trying to keep warm while they wait for the start. Runners in the shirt of their chosen running club or charity, some in new sports kit they've bought for the occasion, others who look like they've pulled on a t-shirt and shorts to go down to the beach and, of course, those running in fancy dress.

There will be spectators too, holding bags for those they've come to cheer on and perhaps holding a camera to get a few snaps as they run past. Kids with banners on which they've written "Go Mum" or "You can do it Dad" stand patiently waiting for the gun and marshals who've given up their Sunday lie-in to come down and help make the event happen are ready with a smile.

There's a divide on race morning between those who are running and those that aren't. For all the encouragement that the officials, supporters and those just going about their business and have stumbled upon the race might give you, they can't run it for you. Their "good luck" and "see you at the finish" are useless if you haven't put in the training. When the voice on the loud speaker calls runners to the start and you wave goodbye to your supporters to line up shoulder to shoulder with strangers, you stand together as both comrades and competitors.

It was almost exactly a year after completing my first 10k race that I lined up for my first half-marathon. I had planned to carry on upping my mileage over the winter and do a half in the spring six months earlier, and I had even entered the Silverstone Half Marathon which took place in March. I had been so enthusiastic to take part in this race that I kept checking the race website to see if it was open for entries yet and entered almost as soon as it had. But after Christmas I got a cold that had lingered and then I went on holiday for two weeks. By the start of February I had hardly run at all so far that year. I wanted to do well in my first half-marathon and not rush through my training, so I decided to DNS ("did not start") and find a race later in the year. In the meantime I did another 10k, the spring Wimbledon 10k in March. I had assumed that with another six months of running in my legs, despite the break from training, I would be certain of a PB. I did manage to finish 40 seconds quicker than the previous 10k, but I suffered for each and every one of those seconds. From halfway I had to stop about five times for a 20-second walking break because my legs couldn't keep up with the rest of my body – something I hadn't had to do the first time round. It wasn't fun and for most of the last four kilometres I was questioning why I'd put myself through it all again. The race wasn't completely without its highlights though.

As I approached the eight kilometre mark a guy ran up alongside me and said: "Excuse me, how long have you been running for?"

"Oh, about a year now," was my reply. He must have been impressed by my pace or style and wanting some tips, I thought!

"No I meant today – my watch has stopped."

There was me thinking he was after a bit of friendly chat and advice but in fact he wanted to know if he was on for finishing in under an hour. It made me chuckle for a good few metres before I went back to thinking about how much my legs hurt. When I crossed the finish line, the thought of doing a half-marathon – more than twice the distance I had just run – seemed ludicrous. But I signed up for one anyway.

So in October 2009, I waited with thousands of other runners for the Great Eastern Run to get underway. The race was in my home town of Peterborough so I was guaranteed two things: no hills this time and plenty of home crowd support. My parents dropped me off at the start and then made their way out to around four miles. When I passed them they were jumping up and down waving and shouting my name. I gave them a wave and picked up my pace as I passed – I was feeling pretty good. I had experimented with energy gels in training and decided they might help give me a boost on the half-marathon. So every five miles I tore open a sachet of energy gel and tried to suck it down. Not all energy gels are the same and the brand I had taken with me were very sickly sweet and hard to swallow. If I had experimented some more before the race I would have found other brands that worked better for me, but this wasn't the case. Around mile ten I saw my parents again. They were still smiling and waving, I on the other hand was not looking so fresh. The second gel went down and my stomach started to complain. Most of the last three miles were run struggling to stay upright as my stomach urged me to bend over and grab my knees. Time didn't matter now, the only thing that mattered was getting to the finish and not stopping until I got there.

With less than half a mile to go I could hear the finishing announcer over the public address system. I knew I was going to make it. As I entered the field where the finish line was, barriers on each side were lined with spectators cheering and clapping. I scanned the crowd along the last 100 metres and found my family urging me on. I looked up at the finish clock, and headed towards the line. I crossed it to complete my first half-marathon in two hours and four minutes. My stomach was sore, my legs were sore and I was exhausted, but I knew I was going to do it all over again. Those four minutes were taunting me and I was so close to the magical two hour mark that I had no choice but to carry training on and try to knock them off.

A year later I returned to Peterborough for the Great Eastern Run with more miles under my belt courtesy of a marathon and more experience in pacing and race nutrition – I wouldn't be making the same mistake with the gels as I had the year before. I was ready to knock those vital four minutes off my

PB to finish in under four hours and this time I had a couple of friends to help me.

My elder brother, who cheered me on in my school sports day, had a friend, Neil, who I've known since I was a kid. He trains with a local running club and was a regular at the Great Eastern Run. He was nursing an injured knee but was aiming to finish under two hours. He and a friend of his had offered to run with me and set a pace that would get us round the course in under two hours.

As we ran around the course we had multiple cheering squads: my parent who, with a year's cheering experience under their belt, managed to catch us at three locations before the finish, as well as Neil's wife and son who popped up a couple of times. Somewhere around eight miles, Neil's knee got the better of him. His mate was starting to fade too, a dodgy ankle hampering his efforts. At around the same time a club-mate of theirs was passing us and slowed to exchange encouragement with Neil and his friend.

"Will you take Laura with you? She wants to finish under two hours. Get her to the finish."

"Sure. No problem."

Neil and his friend dropped off the pace and I continued with their friend, whose name I don't think I caught. We ran together for the next few miles, me conscious that I was slowing him down. As we came into the last mile I turned to him: "Don't worry, you don't have to be gentlemanly, feel free to sprint for the finish."

"I haven't got a sprint finish left in me."

With half a mile to go he urged me on ahead and I waved goodbye: "I'll see you at the finish."

I kept glancing down at my watch, re-checking the maths to confirm that I was going to do it – I was going to finish in under two hours. On the finishing straight I saw my parents again. My dad, shouting "run through the line", was clearly watching the race clock and not aware of the time on my watch. I couldn't have predicted as I calculated my mile splits on the Friday evening before the race that I would manage sub-nine minute miles and achieve a new half-marathon PB of one hour 56 minutes and 31 seconds. I was elated. I waited around to see Neil and his mate finish and to thank them for their pacing. I had never run with others before and had been nervous about it before the start – what if I slowed them down, what if I couldn't keep up? And now I felt a bit guilty – had pacing me to a sub-two time cost them their own race? Runners understand the importance attached to getting a certain race time, and sometimes they're willing to forgo their own race plan to help someone else achieve theirs. I was grateful that they'd helped me that day, and I'd pay the favour forward to another runner at another race another day. And in doing so I would learn that it's just as much fun helping someone else reach their goals as it is to achieve your own.

The following October Neil and myself would be reunited at the start of the 2011 Great Eastern Run and this year we were joined by another friend of his, called Steve. Neil would have a dodgy knee still, Steve a dodgy ankle and I would have a cold that had seen me spend most of the week in bed. Until the morning of the race I hadn't known whether I'd do the run or not.

Between the three of us we had just about enough working body parts and good health to make one fully functioning runner. We were a rag-tag band of runners, but we'd decided to set off together and see what happened. Around mile ten, Neil who was calling out our mile splits and setting the pace decided that sub-two hours was possible. From where I was it seemed a big ask. But we carried on for the last three miles, this time sticking together. As we approached the home straight the three of us all held hands and crossed the finish line together. We had nipped in just under two hours at one hour 58 minutes and it felt just as big an achievement as the year before. "See you next year then," we agreed.

What I wish I had known then

Choosing a race to take part in can be a complex business. I've spent many hours trawling through race listings and reviews to find something that's right for me. It takes almost as much energy as booking a holiday. Whether it's your first ever race or your first attempt at a specific distance, here are a few things to consider when finding a race.

Location

This isn't just a question of what you'll see as you run round on the day, but whether you'll see the start at all. Getting to a start line can be stressful. Think about the logistics of where your race is and how you might get to the start, hopefully without getting up before the sun is up.

Support

Do you need cheering crowds all the way round to keep you going, or will a few friendly marshals suffice? And what about friends and family – will they really want to travel all the way to the North Pole to watch you run?

Cost

Handing over the (sometimes huge) entry fee isn't the only cost involved. If you are looking at a race that's not on your doorstep you could be looking at paying for accommodation, travel and pre-race carb-rich meals out the night before as well. And if you're taking friends and family with you for support, it can get very pricey, very quickly.

Course

Whether you're looking for a PB, are just happy to get round or are looking for a bigger challenge, take a look at the terrain and the hills that you might be tackling on the day. You can usually find an elevation profile for races online and they may just make you question whether the Everest marathon is right for you after all. Think about what's important for you – do you want to run through nice countryside so you can look at the view but where you might not get as much crowd support? Or maybe you can put up with less idyllic surroundings of residential areas and city centres if they bring with them a good turn out from cheering spectators.

Chapter 6

One of us – Joining a running club

"WHY don't you join a running club?" asked the boyfriend.

"Because I'm like Groucho Marx. I refuse to be part of a club that will have me as a member. Also I'm shy and slow and I don't like organised exercise of any kind."

"But winter is coming, it's getting dark – won't you be safer running in a group?"

"I'm perfectly safe by myself. I have a neon jacket you can see from space and I'm reclaiming the streets. You can't live in fear."

This conversation happened a few times. The question of whether or not I should join a running club went back and forth in my mind. I could see the plus points of organised runs: coaches that know what they're talking about and people to support you. But I had never been good with new people, I don't like a crowd and I am generally a bit anti-social – who would have suspected such traits from someone who wrote a blog? I liked the idea of being part of a running club in principle, but in practice I was worried it might trigger flashbacks to PE classes at secondary school and make me revert to my old ways of sitting on the bench faking a sprained ankle.

One of the things I like about running is that it only needs me and a pair of trainers to make it happen. Bring more people into the equation and who knows what might happen. I carried on running because, compared to the me of 12 months earlier, I could see I was actually quite good at it. There was, in my mind though, a real danger that if I ran with people that had been doing it longer or more regularly than myself, I might discover I wasn't that good after all, become disheartened and give up.

But after running the Great Eastern Run with club runners and experiencing the camaraderie between them, I started to rethink my position. I spent a lot of time on the website of the local running club, the Wimbledon Windmillers, checking out their different training sessions, looking at their members' times in local races and convincing myself that I wouldn't show myself up if I turned up to train with them. I had done a few races now and was starting to consider myself a 'real runner' but people that were members of a running club were 'good runners' surely. And I definitely didn't think of myself as a 'good runner'.

I had seen members of the local club when I was out running. When I would stop at the windmill on Wimbledon Common to use the toilets mid-run on a weekend, they were usually sat around having finished their group run enjoying a coffee and some cake. I would regularly run ten miles on a weekend by myself, and I liked to do it on my terms which usually involved waking up about 10am, having a few cups of tea and a big breakfast, watching a few episodes of *Frasier* and then contemplating getting my kit on somewhere after midday. These guys met up and started running before I was even out of bed – that wasn't going to work for me. I had sacrificed a lot of things to running by now: my toenails and my aversion to wearing lycra in public to name just two. I wasn't prepared to give up my weekend lie-ins as well. Running was the easiest sport to fit into my life, I could do it anywhere, any time and on my terms. Why complicate that?

On Tuesday and Thursday nights the club gathered to do hill training and speed sessions meeting up at the same rugby pitch where I had started my first 10k. Hill training and speed session weren't two phrases that regularly came out of my mouth – they sounded hideous. But they did sound like something I should be doing if I wanted to be a 'real runner'. So one dark November evening I climbed on to my bike and cycled to the clubhouse ready to sign up. There were only a few people sat around when I arrived so I took my time locking up my bike, going to the bathroom and then changing out of my cycle clothes. I sat down on one of the benches, texting on my phone and hoping that nobody would talk to me. One of the coaches came over and introduced himself, explained what would be happening (we would be running fast in circles) and asked about my running pedigree.

"I've not been running very long. Only 18 months. I did a half-marathon a few weeks back and haven't really run since then."

"Well you shouldn't have a problem keeping up, but take it easy on the speed as it's your first time and see how you get on."

More people arrived and after some brief announcements about club races, kit and social events, the group was split into two: the faster group and the slower group, and then we all headed off. I joined the slower group, worried that this (as far as I was concerned) would be false advertising and that I would be left for dust, and we ran around the streets of Wimbledon to a predetermined location to run speed intervals down some quiet streets. I can't remember what my first session with the club consisted off but it was probably around a 500m round-the-block route with 400 of those metres being run hard and the last 100m being walked and jogged as a recovery. This would have been done about five times before we took a break and the repeated it in the opposite direction. Surprisingly I wasn't the slowest person there which boosted my confidence and made me think maybe I was a running club type of person after all.

Running fast in circles like this is something that I wouldn't have done by myself on a regular Tuesday evening. The motivation to push yourself ten times to run fast over the same ground is much easier to find when there are 20 other people around you doing the same thing. I joined up and after a few months I got to know a few faces that I would say hello to and I found my place in the pack. I did the speed sessions on Tuesday and the hill sessions on Thursdays, not on the same week though. I was now running up and down the hill that had intimidated me as I had trained for my first race several times in one training run. What's more, after a while I was regularly running at the front of the slower group with the same group of runners and we would push each other on to go that little bit faster than we would have on our own.

When I moved away from Wimbledon, I missed training with the club. Speed sessions were harder to do by yourself so they dropped out of my training diary. Now living in central London I wasn't close to any hills either and I missed that element of training. The feeling that your lungs and thighs might explode followed by relief and calm as you crest the top of a hill – strange as it sounds, I longed for that. I didn't miss it enough to catch the train 20 minutes out to Wimbledon on a Thursday night, but I did miss it.

Eventually I joined the Serpentine Running Club and became a Serpie – despite the club colours being red and yellow which clashed hugely with my ginger hair. Serpentine are a much bigger club which meant training sessions on practically every day of the week that I could go to (or not go to). Not long after joining I had my first experience of running in the club colours in a 10k and then a half-marathon which generated shouts of "go on Serpie" from spectators who were there to support other members.

Training with a running club has made me run faster and brought me into contact with a lot of different people who all have the same interest as me. While friends and family might glaze over as I talk about what races I've done or would like to do, here is a group that listens enthusiastically and have useful advice like "that's my PB course" or "it's a lot hillier than the website describes". People that, instead of saying "are you sure you should be running a marathon? It's bad for your knees" say "I've run ten marathons this year – I love it, go for it". And we all need as much of that sort of encouragement as we can get – as I found out training for my first marathon.

What I wish I had known then

Running clubs aren't everyone's cup of tea, but here are a few things you should know about running with a club to help you make up your mind. I was adamant for a long time that running clubs weren't for me – but then I tried one and found I became a lot faster very quickly.

You'll get expert help
Coaches aren't just for elite athletes. All running clubs have coaches with a range of experience that will be able to help you with training, injury and all sorts of advice. They'll run structured training sessions and give you encouragement.

You'll run faster
We run faster when we run in front of others, whether that's spectators who have come to watch you in a race, the competitors you're running against or just other people out for their Sunday run in the park. So training with others will make you run a bit faster without necessarily realising it.

They're generally friendly places
Everyone is there to run. Whether they run at the front of the pack or the back of the pack, I've found everyone to be encouraging. And, as you have a shared interest in running – even if you're not there to broaden your social circle – you always have that to chat about.

They're not just for super-speedy runners
Maybe you've been put off joining a club by seeing super-fast people in their club shirts at races. Not all club runners are fast. I guarantee that there will be at least one person at any given club that is slower than you or that at least was slower than you when they started.

It's nice to race for a club, but you don't have to
There will usually be someone doing a race that you're thinking of doing and that is maybe aiming to run it at your pace. Running with club runners was how I managed to break two hours in a half-marathon the first time – a couple of club runners I knew paced me through it and kept me going.

Running in club colours usually gets you a few shouts of encouragement as you run round from the friends and family of your team-mates too.

You don't have to go to every session
Looking at some running club schedules can be a bit

overwhelming, but you don't have to go to every single one and very few people actually do.

What to do now
If you're thinking of joining a club, e-mail the secretary or one of the coaches and tell them what sort of running you're currently doing. They'll be able to tell you which sessions might be best for you to go along to first and you'll be able to try them out before you sign up.

Chapter 7

Going the distance – Training for the marathon

I FELL out of bed early (and hungover) one Sunday morning in April 2009 to watch the London Marathon coverage on TV. During the hour or so of build-up the BBC shows before any actual running get underway, I found myself getting quite emotional at people's stories about why they were running. Some of them had overcome serious illness or injury and were now fit and well enough to run 26.2 miles, others were running in memory of a loved one – the pain they were expecting to experience running the race insignificant in comparison to their loss. Some foolhardy souls had decided to make the challenge even tougher, running in costume as a rhino or carrying an oboe. I had memories of watching the London Marathon as a child trying to spot my uncle in his bright yellow running top. Every time someone wearing that neon shade went past the camera we would shout "is that uncle Steve?" But we never spotted him.

The women's elite race got underway and an epic battle between British runner Mara Yamauchi and a Germany's Irina Mikitenko had me gripped. Yamauchi eventually came in two hours later a noble second to Mikitenko. At this point I was exhausted from watching so much running so I went back to bed for a little nap. A couple of hours later I headed into town to watch the back of the pack runners pass the 26-mile mark along the Embankment. I had lived in London for about four years at this stage but I had never seen the London Marathon in real life before and it was pretty spectacular. The emotion I felt just watching people get to the point where they knew they were going to be able to finish reaffirmed for me the fact that I wanted to do a marathon, despite the fact that at this point I still hadn't yet run half of one yet. I carried on clapping and cheering for an hour or two before going home excited that that was going to be me one day. The next morning, when the ballot for the London Marathon 2010 opened, the website promptly crashed under the demand to register. Just getting into this race was going to be a challenge in itself. I tried again throughout the day but with no joy so I set my alarm for the early hours of the next morning (something that would become somewhat of a ritual over the next few years), woke up in the middle of the night when nobody else was online, registered and went back to sleep.

There's three main ways to get a place in the London Marathon. You either run fast and qualify as an 'elite' or 'good for age' runner, get a place via a charity which means agreeing to raise around £2,000 for them or you cross your fingers and try your changes on the ballot. The first two options aren't something everyone can take advantage of because their speed or financial situation won't allow it. So every year around 150,000 people enter the ballot for the London Marathon as I had. Only 50,000 people are lucky enough to actually get a place in the race with even less obtaining their place through the ballot system (a lot of those places are gained through the charity route). Each October when the results of the ballot are announced, more than 120,000 people are disappointed or relieved to receive a rejection letter, and possibly the infamous oversized 'reject jacket'. Looking at the chances of getting a place in this oversubscribed event, I realised that my plan to run London may have been at odds with my newly formed plan to run a marathon before my 30th birthday, even though at this point I was 27. in the same week that I completed my first half-marathon I was one of those 120,000 disappointed people and my "small" reject jacket fitted my dad who usually takes an extra large.

I was disappointed on two counts. As far as I was concerned, the London Marathon was *the* marathon. But as much as the TV coverage of sport might lead you to believe that London Marathon is the only 26.2-mile race happening in the UK every year, this isn't actually the case. All over the country most weekends throughout the year from Loch Ness to Cornwall, runners are lining up in their thousands to run a marathon. By the time I got my rejection letter I had decided that 2010 was going to be the year I did my first marathon, and coincidentally Brighton had done the same. The town would hold its first ever marathon in April 2010, just a week before the London Marathon, which seemed appropriate for me. We were both marathon virgins not knowing what to expect but hoping for the best. I was sold. So in October 2009 I took a deep breath, punched in my credit card details and signed up. That was the easy part.

Training for Brighton started in January 2010, which just happened to be one of the coldest winters on record. Jack Frost had arrived in London. Presumably he didn't use public transport because that was letting us down. The temperature plummeted to minus ten degrees and airports across the country closed their runways. This was not a good start. As I ran down the Thames at lunchtime I expected to see people in Victorian dress skating across its frozen surface. It was pretty cold. I would like to say I sprang out of bed in one joyful bound into my trainers on the first day of marathon training, but that would be a lie. I was still trying to shake off a cold which was making the left side of my face ache and when the alarm went off at 6.10am, I didn't want to go anywhere other than back to sleep. But I got up and felt like both a hero and a victim as I plodded round the streets wearing my high-visibility gear in complete darkness. It always surprises me how many other people are up and already starting their day when I get up earlier than usual. It seems even weirder when it's dark. The busses were already half full and the traffic was steady. The number of other runners I counted though was just four that morning. We all gave each other a smile and a nod that said "why are we doing this?" and knew the answer – we all had marathons to train for.

Marathon training continued through snow and ice, and through a holiday to the Canary Islands. The mileage had been steadily climbing and the weeks had been ticked off. It was only as I came into week eight, however, that my distance headed into the unknown. The furthest I had ever run at this point was 13.1 miles and that was during the Great Eastern Run half-marathon six months earlier. The longest I had run since then was the 12 miles I ran the previous weekend of marathon training. But now I had to head into the unknown and run 14 miles in one go, by myself. The reassuring familiarity of the numbers on the training plan had ended. The friendly 8s, 10s and 12s had gone and were replaced by daunting 14s, 16s and 18s. This was quite a milestone as it marked the end of me being able to say to myself: "It's fine – you can do it, you've done it before."

I acquired some new kit in the shape of a running backpack that had a 'bladder' in it that you can fill with water and drink through a tube. I took it out with me on my longer runs along with my energy gels, which I knew from past experience to test out before race day. I had a couple of pockets in my backpack big enough to carry my phone, Oyster card and some money – three things that would get me safely back home if the run took a turn for the worse.

When I first started running I had no comprehension of the amount of training it would take to run a marathon and how much time it would take up. Runs at the weekend meant hours spent running around in the cold followed by the rest of the day recovering on the sofa. During the week I would run up and down the River Thames at lunchtime, if I could fit in a shorter run before rushing back to my desk. If I had to run further than four miles I had to run after work. It was cold and dark by the time I'd leave my office at 5.30pm but I would put on my hat and gloves, my running tights and a high-visibility jacket and I'd run home or part of the way home before jumping on the tube. I had started to enjoy running, but training for the marathon was sometimes a chore – my legs were usually still tired for my previous run and the miles didn't always come easily. Even a three-mile run, a distance I had been able to run for nearly two years, could make me suffer as much as it had on those first runs on the treadmill if my legs were still tight or sore from the weekend's long run. But every time I zipped up my jacket and headed out I was moving a little bit closer towards my goal. It felt good at the end knowing I could tick another run off my schedule and that I was gradually working my way towards the marathon finish line.

I'm not sure that many non-runners have much of an idea of the hours involved in training for a marathon. My friends and family certainly didn't before I started turning down invites because I had to run and the possibility of a spontaneous 'quick drink after work' disappeared in favour of a six-mile run in the dark.

On some of my runs I had company: my friend Phil would cycle alongside me chatting away to me. Sometimes he would listen to his latest podcast while I would listen to my music and I would just feel reassured that he was there. Sometimes he would get bored by the slow pace and cycle off for a while then loop back and rejoin me. My dad too has joined me on long marathon training runs, cycling ahead to open gates for me so I didn't have to stop and shouting out my mile splits and calculating my speed, his ability to do complex calculations while exercise far better than mine. Despite my history as one of the laziest, inactive teenagers you could image, none of my friends or family batted an eyelid when I announced I was going to run a marathon. If they thought I couldn't do it or that I would give up on training they kept it hidden well because I've only ever had support from them.

There have been negative people who have said unhelpful things to me such as "all that running is bad for your knees", "it's not good for you running a marathon" or "don't you find running boring though". On these occasions I smile politely and try to change the conversation. People that know me have seen how much happier, how much more confident and how healthier I am because of running. And those that care about me wouldn't dream of discouraging me from doing something that makes me happier, more confident and healthier.

As I approached the final weeks of big mileage, my training plan called for two 18-mile runs a week apart. Thirteen weeks earlier when I started training the idea of running 18 miles by myself round Richmond Park seemed ludicrous. I couldn't comprehend it ever being possible and it seemed like an even bigger challenge than running the marathon itself. I found myself in a pub one Wednesday night, two days after my first 18-mile run. It was a work leaving do and I was drinking sparkling water wondering how long I had to hang around before I could go home. I got talking to the wife of one of my former colleagues who had just taken up running herself. She was training to run 10k and was finding running for a few miles a challenge. She listened with interest when I told her about my training and then asked how far I had run at the weekend.

"I ran 18 miles last weekend and I have to run 18 miles again this weekend."

"You ran 18 miles? That's amazing."

"Yeah it's a bit surreal for me to think about it."

"Wow, I'm so impressed. I'm going to tell my running group that I met someone who ran for 18 miles."

I remember vividly how, for a moment, she made me feel like a superhero. I was in her shoes just 18 months earlier and the idea of running 18 miles solo made my mind boggle. I wanted to run a marathon but as I stared at my training plan I didn't think I'd be able to manage all those miles. But I started out anyway and hoped for the best.

If I had known when I punched in my credit card details and signed up for Brighton Marathon that the UK was set to experience the coldest winter in 31 years, I may have reconsidered. But I didn't, so I couldn't. With all my long runs completed and just 19 days to go before I would be lining up at the start, I tried to remind myself of that. I would have thought I couldn't possibly have trained in such temperatures or conditions as the UK experienced that winter, but I did it. I thought I wouldn't be able to run 18 miles and not collapse in a big heap, but I did it. So I knew that when I lined up at the start line I would probably think to myself "there's no way I can run 26.2 miles".

But I would remind myself that I had proven several times already that year that I am capable of much more than I'd ever thought possible. I have more determination than I had previously thought, and more than enough to keep me going for those extra miles and run a marathon. You're not just training your legs to go the distance but your mind to believe you can do it. At some point in training, you have to stop thinking you won't be able to run a marathon and start believing you can.

What I wish I had known then

Training for a marathon takes a lot of time. Depending on the training plan you choose, you're looking at about four runs a week for around 16 weeks. Gradually the runs will get longer and will take more time. So before you commit, have you got other demands in the next four months that will need your full attention? If you have, maybe now isn't the best time for you.

There are lots of marathons taking place all over the UK every year and, despite being the biggest, London may not be the best for you. An autumn marathon may fit better around other commitments you have during the year and would mean the evenings are brighter for your mid-week training runs.

It requires some creativity, but runs can be fitted into your social life or around other commitments. Running home from work or at lunchtime are just two way to make it work for you. Running to a friend's house for dinner or running to the supermarket before doing the weekly shop are ways that I've got round keeping my life going during marathon training. And if all else fails, it's time to set the alarm early and do the miles before the day even gets started.

It's not just about doing the miles though, during marathon training it's important to get enough sleep and eat well. Because if you're tired and skipping breakfast it will make your runs much tougher and you won't recover as well after them. So even on days when I didn't have runs planned, I found myself heading home early from social occasions to get an early night so I could be ready for running the next morning.

If you're questioning whether you should do a marathon or not then the answer is, probably, yes you should. You'll always wonder if you don't at least try. But there's no rush – there's no time limit on how long after starting running you can leave it before you sign up for one and there's no upper age cap on entry, so if you're not ready wait a while. The more experience you have of running before you start training for a marathon the more enjoyable you'll find it – and you might even make some running buddies along the way to train with.

You don't have to do a marathon just because everyone you know that runs has done one or because people keep asking you if you've done one. You don't get a special card or become a 'proper runner' because you've done a marathon. In fact a lot of people do marathons and then give up running. So if it doesn't appeal to you – don't worry about it. Concentrate on the things you enjoy and the challenges that push you.

Chapter 8

Trick of the mind – The mental aspect of running

'VE been overtaken while running quite a bit. Mostly I tell myself "they're probably not going as far as me" which tends to do the trick and makes me feel better about being slower than whoever this is. But that doesn't always work though. One morning I was out running round Richmond Park – one of my favourite places to run. There are miles of paths to run along and herds of deer roaming free. I was training for marathon number one and doing a long run. As I got towards one of the gates a group of kids around 15 years old were stood around. I stopped to use the toilets and when I came out they were getting ready to start running. They didn't look like they ran very much, they all wore fashion trainers and tracksuit bottoms on what was quite a sunny day. I resumed my run and after about 100 metres they started to over take me. First a couple of fast boys racing each other and then more of them until eventually all of about 20 kids had run past me.

My competitive juices started and I picked up my pace a little. I had been overtaken by people that I had looked at and judged I should be running faster than and this bugged me. Soon after the public toilets at Sheen Gate, as you head towards Richmond Gate, there's a long gradual hill that can sap your energy and as I approached it I saw that a few of these kids had started walking along this uphill stretch. I overtook three of them – some of them panting loudly, one with their hand pressed against their stomach, the tell-tale sign of a stitch – and I was feeling quite pleased with myself and looked for more. On what is quite a hilly part of the park I overtook all but the first two fast boys and by now I was gunning for this pair. I could see them ahead of me and I'd made myself the mental challenge to catch them by the next gate. As we approached Richmond Gate they were just ten metres in front of me – that was enough for them to cross the road and leave me waiting for the traffic to pass. I caught up with them a few minutes later as I passed a cafe where they had met their teacher or youth leader. They were panting, out of breath and having a drink waiting for the rest of their friends. Their run was over, but I still had another lap of the park to do before heading home to bring my run up to 16 miles.

I had compared myself to these kids and judged that I should be able to run faster than them. It had bothered me that they had been able to drop me so quickly and I had got competitive. In doing so I had forgotten the plan I'd set for my own run. I had forgotten the pace I was trying to keep and that I still had more than ten miles left to run, and in doing so I'd put the rest of my run in jeopardy by getting caught up in a race that was only happening in my own head. These kids could probably beat me over a few hundred metres but over a marathon I would probably win. But what does any of that matter? When I compete in races, a lot of people finish behind me – but if the time I see on the clock when I finish isn't a time I'm proud of I'll be unhappy for the rest of the day. The opposite is true – it doesn't matter how many people finish in front of me, if I get a PB it's like winning my own personal race.

The following week as I was doing the second of my 16-mile runs in preparation for my first marathon. I stopped at a set of traffic lights at around mile 11 and I stopped my Garmin stopwatch which was measuring the time and distance I'd run for. I got about half a mile further down the road and looked down at my Garmin only to see that I had forgotten to press 'start' again. For the remaining few miles of my run I obsessed about how far I had run while my watch was stopped. It was a new route and I hadn't plotted all 16 miles before I set off, so I was relying on my Garmin to get all of the 16 miles in. But now I didn't know how far I'd run and this caused me a huge amount of anxiety when, really it shouldn't have. I was fretting over doing exactly 16 miles as though 15.5 or 16.3 would mean disaster. I estimated how far I thought my watch had been stopped for and mentally added that to the total showing on the watch face. I guessed it to be about half a mile and that should have been enough for me to forget about it and finish my run (it was pretty accurate too as I later calculated), but I worried about it for the remaining miles. When you've run that far and your body and mind are tired, little things can somehow become a huge deal. Needless to say I didn't have a pleasant run for the remaining miles but a lesson had been learned. Not only to remember to press 'start' but to relax when things don't go to plan.

These two runs taught me important lessons that I would take with me into races with me. In the grand scheme of things, a forgotten piece of kit or an unmeasured half-mile rarely matters. But worrying about the small things in a big way can actually start to affect your performance and, more importantly, your enjoyment of a race. If I forgot my watch one day and turned up to the start of a race without it I would probably freak out and panic, but really there wouldn't be anything I could do. I would have to improvise, trust how I felt as an indicator of how fast I was running and focus on the race.

Likewise, racing those school children during my 16-mile run was a foolish thing to do, but its something that can happen all too easily in a race. When I go into a race of any distance, I have a plan for how I want to approach it. Sometimes I want a PB and I know exactly how fast I need to run each mile in order to finish on target. Getting caught up in a race with other runners or going faster because you see someone that you judge *should* be slower than you is a mistake that it's all too easy to make. You need to stick to your own race plan and forget about what everyone around you is doing. It's common in races for people to start out running too fast.

Either they've judged their pace or target poorly or they want to get away from all the crowds at the start. Ignore what everyone else is doing and go at your own pace. Going out too fast will, even if you feel good at the time, will leave you suffering in the later stages.

I like to image all the runners rushing past me at the start of the race as the tide going out. Eventually that tide will start to come back in again as, in the second half of races, I often find myself passing people who have slowed or begun to walk.

What I wish I had known then

There are a few mental techniques I've found that can help when it comes to running.

Break it down

If you're worried about running a long way in a race or a training run, don't think about the whole distance – think of it in sections. For me a marathon is four sections of five miles and then a 10k at the end. At the end of each five-mile section I have an energy gel and I try to stop myself from thinking of miles that aren't in the section I'm currently running. So from miles ten to 15, I'm not allowed to think about anything beyond mile 15.

Positive thoughts

Positive self-talk can really help when the going gets tough. Figure out some mantras that work for you beforehand. These are just positive thoughts that you repeat over and over again in your mind. Things that have worked for me include "yes I can, yes I can, yes I can". Or "feeling good, feeling strong, feeling good, feeling strong". Repeat them enough and you start to believe them. They take a bit of practice but they can help.

Smile

Smiling helps in races. If I see a camera, and there are generally a lot of them, I smile at it. It reminds me that what I'm doing is a hobby, not something I'm being forced to do. I imagine looking at the photo that has just been taken and how proud I'll be looking back on this moment. This also reminds me that, as much as it feels like it at times, this run won't go on forever – it will finish at some point.

Let's pretend

I'm not too embarrassed to admit that sometimes, when I'm really struggling on a long run, I imagine myself in the Olympic games with just a few laps of the track to go to claim gold, or that I'm running the last few miles of the London Marathon in second place and that, if I really try, I can break the tape in first. I imagine the commentary, I imagine my competitors and more often than not, my legs start moving that little bit faster.

Chapter 9

The big one – Running the marathon

DURING the day and hours before the race I was really nervous. If anyone asked me what I was specifically worried about, I couldn't answer. All I knew was that I was nervous. I checked into the glamorous venue of the Preston Park Travelodge in Brighton the night before the race. Budget, no-frills accommodation was to feature in much of my marathon experiences. It was basic but only a couple of hundred metres from the start and that was what mattered most to me that day. I left my hotel room at 8.30am to go to the start and as soon as I got in the queue for the toilets (despite having just used the toilet in my room) my nerves started to subside. Fifteen minutes later the queue for the toilet still wasn't moving so I found a handy bush to go behind and then lined up with the thousands of other runners, waiting for the off.

The start was delayed by about 20 minutes and by the time the gun went off everyone in the field had gone from feelings of dread to being eager to get going. I didn't spot my friend Phil who had come along and who was dutifully waiting to see me cross the line, and he didn't see me but on later inspection of the video evidence it seems that I ran straight past him. For the first couple of miles a man dressed as Mr Potatohead ran behind me. I couldn't see him but all I could hear as I ran along were spectators shouting "go on Mr Potatohead". I had put my name on my vest as advised by many a veteran marathon-runner so that the crowd would cheer me on by name – but Mr Potatohead was deflecting attention away from me and I'd need as much support as I could get. Eventually Mr Potatohead's costume started to weigh him down and his pace slowed allowing me to leave my starchy rival behind by mile three and pick up a few people shouting "go on Laura".

I had arranged to see Phil at mile five, but the mile marker came and went with no familiar face to cheer me on. This added to not seeing him at the start began to get me down, but I tried to focus on the race and not to get worked up about it as I set off on my way out of Brighton along the coast. The next few miles ticked by without any major difficulty and I diligently took my energy gels every five miles as planned. Around nine miles I decided a toilet stop was in order, but the queues put me off. So I did as the men were and found an alternative spot. Not long after leaving the route turned around and headed back into Brighton. I could see the pier and with it the halfway mark ahead of me.

As I went through halfway I was feeling good, but I still had half the race to go. Then I saw Phil who jumped out of the crowd at me shouting my name and almost immediately my stride got quicker. I had decided that a ten-minute-mile pace was achievable. It was the speed I had managed to maintain for my 18-mile training run and I hoped that I would be able to hold close to it for the whole 26.2. I didn't know what would happen after 18 miles but my aim was to finish in under five hours. I didn't notice the 18-mile marker as I ran past it, which was probably a good thing. I had now run further than I had ever run before without realising it and by the time I got to 19 miles I had seen a couple of friends and was feeling as good as I believe you can after running that far.

The route took us on a long slog out to a power station and it was a difficult, desolate section. Not being a local helped. I just kept running without knowing how far it was to the turnaround that would put me on the home straight. By this point I was passing quite a few people that were walking. If my first aim was to finish in under five hours, my second aim was not to walk a single step. I kept plodding on, past the people who were limping, past people sat by the side of the road stretching and past the man in the gorilla costume that he'd probably decided, in hindsight, wasn't such a good idea on a day that topped 20 degrees. I kept waiting to hit 'the wall'. I had heard it was strong possibility. But there was no wall for me, other than the physical one that the route organisers had erected at around 22 miles for us to run through. I was, however, getting a stomach ache and the bumbag I was wearing was pressing on my stomach with every step and making it worse.

So what else was I to do but take it off and sling it over my shoulder like a handbag? I laughed to myself as I ran along. Apparently marathon legend Haile Gebrselassie runs with one arm crooked because he used to run to school every day carrying his school books in that arm. I imagined that there was some affinity between myself in the great man at that moment. In reality I probably looked like I do while running for the train clutching my handbag on the way to work, not an elite Ethiopian marathon runner.

At around mile 23 Brighton Pier became visible in the distance, marking with it the finish area. As we ran along the seafront the crowd was thick on both sides with spectators who were loud in their support. It was like running through a tunnel, and all I could see was the end and a blur of faces on both sides. I counted down the miles and told myself "half an hour and it's all over", "20 minutes and you can stop", "15 minutes and that's it".

I wondered why I was doing it and I got emotional when I realised that I would make it. I fought back the tears because I didn't want the spectators to think I was in pain or not enjoying it because, as much as I wanted it to end, I was loving every minute. Someone in the crowd shouted "you can do it Laura" and I remember saying out loud to myself "yes, I bloody well can do it".

At mile 25 it was time to put my bumbag back on ready for my finishing picture. My speed picked up and the next thing I knew the sign saying "800m to go" appeared. From then on I was running as fast as my legs could carry me. I took off the cap I had been wearing since the start, ready to face the cameras and, overcome by spectators shouting my name, I threw it into the crowd as though I was Wimbledon champion. It took two years and many hundreds of miles to get there, but on Sunday 18th April 2010 I finished my first marathon.

I crossed the finish line in four hours and 31 minutes exhausted but elated. A volunteer grabbed hold of me, propped me up and walked me to get my medal. He kept talking to me telling me how great I had done and all I kept saying was "you've all been great, the supporters were great". I don't know who he was, or what he looked like because I was looking around at everyone else soaking up the finish, but his hug was much needed and to have someone to share that moment with was fantastic. Thank you Brighton for the support – and thank you to the volunteer who welcomed me into the club of marathoners!

At that moment I knew I was hooked. I wanted to run another marathon, I wanted to run a faster marathon and, although I was delighted to have finished Brighton in four hours and 31 minutes, I wanted to run my next marathon in less than four hours. So after the blisters had healed and the soreness in my legs had subsided I would be out running again and thinking about marathon number two and a sub-four hour time goal. What I didn't know then was quite how long it would take to make that goal a reality.

What I wish I had known then
No new kit
As tempting as it might be to treat yourself to a new outfit for marathon day as a reward for coming so far, don't wear anything for your marathon that you haven't worn without problems on your long run. Chaffing and blisters are not your friends and can pop up in the most unlikely places. Test your kit out before race day and wear something that's comfortable. I hadn't tested out the bumbag that I wore in Brighton and I paid the price. Luckily the bumbag was something I could easily take off when it became a problem, new shoes that were rubbing wouldn't have been so easy to sort out mid-race.

Test your nutrition
Most marathons will give out some sort of sports drink at various points on the course. Find out what brand it is before

race day and test it on your long runs to make sure it doesn't cause you any problems. Not everyone gets on well with all sports drinks and it's best to know in advance so you can take your own if you need to. If you're planning on taking any gels you should test these too before the big day as their effects vary.

Put your name on your shirt

Everyone said the crowd would cheer my name if I did this. But I wasn't expecting quite so many people to be shouting out for me and offering me encouragement from start to finish. It made such a difference both to my motivation and the experience – I felt like a superstar.

Start slow and go slower

Most people running a race (especially a marathon) go off too fast and end up paying for it in the later stages. Don't get dragged along with the masses, plan what pace you're going to run at and stick to it. If, come mile 18, you find you've got something left in the tank – by all means pick up the pace. But something tells me you won't. If you haven't run a race before I recommend doing at least a 5k before your marathon so you can practice sticking to your pace while faster runners whiz past you.

Slow down for water stations

If you need to take a drink, slow down and walk through the water station. It won't make any difference to your time and you're more likely to get your drink in your mouth than up your nose. If you don't need a drink it's still wise to slow down. Thirsty runners can lose all common sense when they approach a drink stop, carelessly throwing unwanted bottles and running into your path to grab a drink. So slow down and take care.

Seeing friends and family

Decide in advance where your friends and family are going to stand to look out for you and tell them to get a big balloon or something to help you spot them but try not to focus too much on seeing them. In a big city marathon it can be pretty tough to find each other and that can be an emotional blow. I missed seeing my friend at the first two of our designated spots and didn't see him until half way which got me down for a couple of miles. Accept in advance that it will be hard to spot them.

Smile for the cameras
There's be so many people taking photos you'll feel like a celebrity. Although you probably won't feel or look your best, in a few weeks you'll be proudly showing strangers on the bus your marathon pictures.

There will probably be the official race photographers as well as snappers from the local paper and you may even find yourself on Flickr courtesy of local amateur photographers as I have. So smile at any cameras pointing at you – even if you don't feel like it.

Remember how far you've come
In the days and minutes before the starting pistol goes off, everyone thinks about what they should or could have done differently. One more long run, a few miles further, another sports massage. By this point, it's too late and instead you should be focussing on what you *have* done. Remember when you thought you'd never get round your long run? Or even when five miles sounded huge? But you did it and you can run a marathon too.

Enjoy it
If it's your first marathon you're guaranteed a PB (PR for the Americans). I know it won't be easy, but that's why you're doing it isn't it? So you can set yourself apart form the 99% of the population that will never run this far. So take in the sights, sounds and atmosphere. Leave the time goals for your next marathon and make finishing with a smile on your face the target.

It's addictive
For some people one marathon, or even no marathons, is enough for them. But for some of us marathon running becomes part of our lives. I've run five marathons now and have a whole lot more on my list of races that I want to do. So watch out – it might just become a habit. But there are worse habits you could develop.

Chapter 10

When nature calls – Toilet training for runners

AFTER completing my fourth Great Eastern Run half-marathon I was celebrating with a group of friends back at a pub. As my dad got in a round of drinks for the thirsty runners I went off to the toilets where I made an unusual discovery. There were leaves in my knickers. At the start of the race where the queue for the Portaloos snaked around the field and never seemed to end, my friends and I took the executive decision to find some foliage where we could discreetly have a wee. They stood guard while I squatted in the shrubbery but in my haste to pull up my bottoms, I had clearly taken part of a bush with me. The leaves had ridden in my bottoms for 13.1 miles before I had noticed them.

Taking up running is a great voyage of discovery that will acquaint you better with yourself, break down the boundaries of what you thought was possible and show you that, if you practice and want it badly enough, you can in fact hold a wee for hours. If you're training for your first race, congratulations because you just got a new best friend in the shape of your toilet habits. You will become obsessed with when you last went, how much you've drunk, what colour your wee is and whether or not you might need to go again in the next hour. New parents and runners are the only people on earth, maybe with the exception of Gillian McKeith, who are this interested in numbers one and two. But this is an important matter and one that is of great concern to a lot of new runners. What if I need the toilet and there's nowhere to go? Why do I always need a 'number two' half way into my run? These are things that can put you off getting out there and running. So I'm going to swallow my pride and share some of my less glamorous running stories with you. Feel free to skip this chapter.

You'll probably have discovered by now that running requires a delicate balance of not being dehydrated, but not being too hydrated before you head out the door. As well as the danger of water sloshing about in your stomach for the next three miles, there's also the danger that you'll need to stop for a toilet break. Most people that have been running for a while will be able to tell you every public convenience, accommodating pub and discreet bush where it's possible to relieve yourself within a good three-mile radius of their house. These aren't the things that you choose to know, you just learn them over time.

Richmond Park is among my favourite places for long runs, not only because it's rare a slice of the countryside within London offering miles of trails, path and road to run on as well as wild deer wandering through it – but also because it has some pretty nice toilets evenly spaced around the perimeter and lots of foliage in between to afford the desperate runner some privacy.

As well as a well practised routine of number ones alfresco, I also employ a technique that I've named 'just bloody hold it'. Now the good thing about running is that many of the skills gained from it cross over into real life situations. For example I once spent six hours on a third-class train from Bangkok to the Cambodian border. The toilet was a hole in the floor of the train, the tracks racing past as you stared down at it. That was a good six hours of 'just bloody hold it' training in action.

Training runs aren't just about improving your fitness and getting miles in your legs, they're also practice sessions for races. So finding out how you'll deal with needing to make a toilet stop during a race will stand you in good stead come race day. Nobody wants to have to stop for a number one on race day and they certainly don't want to stop for a number two. Unlike when you're running for miles on your own in a training run, most longer races have the added benefit of additional toilet facilities laid on just for us runners. But race Portaloos pose two obstacles for the runner: they generally have a long queue and they can be pretty grim. Should you decide to stop for a Portaloo and you have the ability to block out the scenery inside, the queue will not only eat into your time but can make your legs forget how to run and you realise how much it hurts. And don't even think about trying to hover over the seat – the moment your thighs see that Portaloo seat they'll be forcing your arse towards it faster than you can say antiseptic hand gel.

There is, of course, the option to 'do a Paula' as it's known and stop by the roadside. For the record though I've only seen Paula Radcliffe have a wee once in a marathon where as I have done it on no less than five occasions, so maybe this should be named after me instead. More runners have seen my bare arse at the side of the road over the years than have seen an acceptance letter for the London Marathon. In Brighton marathon I stopped for two wees out in the open air. The first was unintentional – I had stopped in a village along the coast at around nine miles where a line of Portaloos had been set up. I had already passed a couple of toilet stops and decided it was too busy so I would carry on running. By the time I reached this village I had no option other than to stop. But the queue was long with other runners. A few metres away there was a patch of grass and some trees. And by the trees was a large commercial bin. I jogged over and behind it, out of the view of the crowds I pulled down my shorts and let go of my inhibitions. As I pulled up my shorts and headed back on to the course a group of women who had spied what I had just done decided to follow my lead. As they passed me one of them shouted over her shoulder to her friends: "Right girls, this is the ladies'."

Ten miles further down the road and full of Powerade and water, I needed to go again. There were seven miles left of the race and that was going to take me at least an hour. I knew that I couldn't hold out that long. This time there were no trees around and I couldn't see any Portaloos either. We were at a point on the course where it heads out to a power station along the coast before turning round and heading back towards the finish. Spectators are few and far between out here and with no support and 19 miles in their legs, runners hate this stretch. A crash barrier by the side of the road would have to take the place of a bush. I squatted behind it, my head and shoulders just visible to the runners going past. I was there less than a minute in total but mid-flow another tired runner decided to take a break and sat down on the crash barrier a meter away from where I was squatted. "Oi mate. A bit of privacy please." He hadn't seen me until I called out, but he turned, saw me and rather embarrassedly (or repulsed) stood up and carried on running.

What I wish I had known then

Toilet training

If you want to avoid getting caught short on a run or during a race, the key is to get your hydration right. If I'm running straight after work I drink a litre of water (plus cups of tea) during the day but stop drinking at least an hour before I head out the door. This ensures I'm hydrated but gives me plenty of time to go to a loo a couple of times before my run and know I won't need to stop along the way.

For races I drink plenty of water the day before to make sure I'm properly hydrated. Then the morning of the race I'll have half a pint of water about an hour and a half before and then that's it for fluids until I'm out on the course. This hydration method works for me, but everyone is different. Pay attention to how much you're drinking and when, and test out what might work for you.

Look out below

A quick and easy way to find out if you're hydrated is to look before you flush. Darker yellow urine mean you need to drink more (or maybe that you recently had a multivitamin – I've be known to forget and get a shock when I look into the toilet bowl), while the clearer your wee the more hydrated you are. It's not rocket science.

Number twos

Nobody wants to have to 'make like a bear' when they're out on a run. Nobody. The way to avoid this is to know what time of day is best for you. I'd love to be able to jump out of bed, pull on my trainers, head out the door and run first thing in the morning, but unfortunately my stomach has other plans for that time of day. I wouldn't get more than two miles before having to answer that, rather important, call of nature. This does, however, mean that on race day, by the time I've had my breakfast and made my way to the start – I'm good to run without interruptions.

Don't be shy

It is possible to get stage fright on race day and not be able to go. So if you think you might need to make an unscheduled stop on race day, practice in training.

Chapter 11

In it together – Running with friends

A S I ran my first marathon in 2010, my oldest friend Katie was waking up with a hangover. This took everyone we knew by surprise. We've been friends since school, catching the same bus to school together each morning. Back then we were polar opposites. While I tried my hardest to skive PE, went out to parties and got drunk at the weekends, Katie was getting driven to and from tennis competitions, winning tennis competitions and beating some of the girls that went on to become some of the top UK women's players.

One summer holiday Katie decided that she was going to change my lazy ways and make a tennis player out of me too. Her plan was to get me good enough that I could return a ball if it was hit pretty much right at me so that I could be her doubles partner in matches that she was undoubtedly good enough to win single-handed. We went down to the tennis court at the local park and she put me through a warm-up that was to consist of a few laps of jogging round the court followed by some stretches. Two laps in and the size of the task Katie had set herself became obvious – not only was I out of breath and had a stitch but I was also complaining about how much everything hurt.

For the sake of our friendship we put down the rackets and went home to watch some MTV together – something I was much better suited to. Needless to say, if anyone had put bets on which of us would have been first to cross the finish line of a marathon, my odds would have offered a much bigger return than hers.

The Friday after finishing the Brighton Marathon I put on a pair of heels for the first time in months and, with weary legs, staggered to Katie's birthday drinks. Despite showing her the damage that had been done to my feet – the black toenails, the blisters, the fact I was still walking like a cowboy – after a few drinks Katie announced: "That's it, I'm going to do a marathon before I'm 30." She had two years in which to do this and cleverly utilised every day of those by leaving it to the very last minute. Her first marathon would also be Brighton and it would take place just six days before her big 3-0. By coincidence, I too had a spot in the 2012 Brighton Marathon after my friend Tim dropped out and deferred his place to me.

I hadn't done a long training run with another runner since the five miles I ran with my friend Rostam in preparation for our first 10k, and that was back when I considered five miles a long run. But one Saturday both Katie and myself were back in our home town of Peterborough and planning to run long, so we headed out together. She ran from her parents' house to mine and then we ran 15 miles around some local lakes before she dropped me off and headed on for her last couple of miles on her own.

For all of those 15 miles we chatted, caught up on gossip – I had been away for four months so there was a lot of this to be caught up on – and kept cover for each other while we relieved ourselves in the local woodland. The miles flew past and, by keeping the pace 'conversational', as in that at which we could still hold a conversation without struggling for breath, we made sure we weren't running too fast.

It was fun having someone to while away the miles with. So fun, in fact, that I offered to pace Katie through the Brighton Marathon – her first and my third marathon. She wanted to finish the marathon in under four hours and 30 minutes and my plan was to run it slower than I was capable of and treat it less as a race and more as a long training run for Edinburgh Marathon which I would be running six weeks later. Katie accepted, 15 miles of my nattering away not putting her off, and so we decided to run together.

Running a marathon at a speed slower than my marathon goal pace was an interesting experience. Before the race I didn't feel nervous. I still had a target to hit to finish in 4.29, and there was the added pressure of not messing up Katie's race, but the morning of the race I felt calm and I stayed relaxed the whole way round. I had told myself before we started that I wasn't allowed to bring any negative chat on to the course with me, so if my legs hurt I couldn't say that out loud, if I was tired I would keep that to myself too and blisters would remain a secret until the finish line. Keeping your head in the right place through 26.2 miles can be difficult. If someone next to you is moaning about how much their feet hurt it makes you start to think about whether or not your own feet hurt and pretty soon your feet are killing you.

As we ran around Brighton I was able to look out for other runners I knew on the route and give them all a cheer. I could soak up the atmosphere: I was able to laugh at the signs that read "Feet hurt? That's because you're kicking so much ass" or "May the course be with you" and "Go complete strangers" then thank the supporters for turning out. I danced with my arms to the music being played along the course and I high-fived every kid that stuck their hand in my direction. I could enjoy the race in a different way than I had the first time I had run Brighton.

We had set out with the aim of running ten-minute miles all the way round, but a couple of toilet and stretching stops had put us behind the pace we needed. A couple of times the 4.30-pacer group overtook us and would have to reel them back in again and get ahead of them to get back on track for our goal finish time. They had started a couple of minutes behind us so we couldn't count on just sticking with the pacer pack to get us to the finish on time. The further you run the more difficult simple arithmetic becomes and calculating the pace that you need to do over the last three miles of a marathon becomes almost impossible in the latter stages of the race, especially if you forget about that all important 0.2 miles. As we approached mile 23 I did the maths several times over. It was going to be very tight for us to dip in under four hours and 30 minutes.

"We need to pick up the pace Katie. It's going to be close." She looked at her watch and nodded, it had been a one-way conversation for the last couple of miles. I picked up the pace and Katie came with me as we weaved through the sea of runners.

Running through the last couple of miles everyone around me was giving it their all to get to the finish line and I felt a bit bad that I was still bounding along quite calmly and, in my mind, stealing cheers that they needed. But that's not to say that running a marathon at a slower pace than you're capable of is easy, because it isn't.

Your energy levels are higher but your feet and legs have still run 26.2 miles and, however fast or slow you run it, that's still pretty far. We saw the sign saying "800 metres to go" and we ran faster. A group of Katie's friends screamed out from the crowd and we waved as we surged past them. We crossed the finish line and looked down at our watches. We'd finished in four hours 29 minutes and 15 seconds. We had cut it fine, but we had done it.

The Brighton Marathon was the most enjoyable 'long run' I've ever done. And helping a friend to achieve their goal was a great feeling. After we crossed the finish line Katie said she'd never do another marathon again: "Been there, done it, don't need to do it again." We'll see about that.

What I wish I had known then
REASONS TO RUN WITH OTHERS
You'll run faster
Run with someone who is faster or a similar speed to you and you'll find yourself picking up the pace. Even the least competitive of people will start to get into race mode and start pushing themselves to go that little bit faster. One lunchtime I went out for a run with a colleague who has similar PB times to me.

When I was struggling to keep up I figured he had been training hard while I'd been away and was now too quick for me. Turns out, much to both our surprises, we had been flying through four miles in around seven and a half minutes per mile pace, which was faster than either of us runs solo.

Subconsciously we would got competitive and gone out faster than either of us intended.

You'll run slower
It's not all about going out fast, sometimes you'll need to slow that pace down for recovery runs or long slow runs. Running with someone slower than you or with someone who is running further than you can help you take your foot off the gas and relax. When I joined Katie on her long run, was running 20 miles. I only needed to do about 15 but I wanted to take it slow. As she was running much further than me I knew the pace would be about right and it was.

You'll stick to your run
Plan to run with another person and you're more likely to stick to your arrangements. Knowing that a friend is waiting at the bus stop for you to start that run you agreed to do with them makes it much harder to turn off the alarm and go back to sleep. Even when it's raining.

Chat and the miles will fly by
Run with an old pal and the run will feel like it's ended before you've even got your trainers on. Catching up on gossip and generally having a good old chin wag does that. And chatting as you go ensures you keep your pace 'conversational' – perfect for long runs.

Misery loves company
You've run for miles. Your legs hurt, your feet hurt and you're unsure where the sweat on your t-shirt ends and the tears begin. You run past endless people having a picnic in the park, enjoying the warm weather and drinking a glass of wine. You hate every single one of them because they're having fun lounging in what, for you, isn't a park but an amphitheatre of pain. But next to you is one person who knows how you feel. They too have staggered through miles of pain and are questioning why they're doing it. You're in this together. Doesn't that make it feel a bit better?

Chapter 12

Disaster strikes – Injury, illness and hypochondria

THEY say Londoners are unfriendly and don't talk to each other, but I beg to differ. I had left my flat and hobbled, hopped and stumbled my way down four flights of stairs, eyes watering from the pain in my right leg as I did so. Out on the street I clutched hold of the wall as I tried bravely to make it to the tube that would deliver me to Guy's Hospital Urgent Care Unit.

"Hurt your back?" came the shout from across the street.

"No, it's my leg," I called back.

"Trapped nerve. The pain's in your leg but the problem's in your back. Put some ice on it."

A GP between house calls perhaps? A physiotherapist on his way to an appointment? Or an off-duty paramedic? He walked towards a bus waiting at a bus stand, put on a high-visibility jacket and climbed behind the wheel. No then, a bus driver.

"Thanks, I'll give it a go." I didn't.

I had hurt my leg the previous night. I had set out to run six miles home from work and the first mile went ok. Then the second mile sort of sucked. By the third mile I was having to take walking breaks – something I hadn't done since I tried to run a half-marathon in the 30-degree heat of Bangkok six months earlier. Weird spasm type feelings that, while not painful, were unsettling and uncomfortable kept pulsing through my leg. I felt like my leg might give way at any point and that I would fall to the ground. So I did what most runners do in this sort of situation: I carried on running.

This was the wrong decision but it's one that runners make every day. I was ten weeks away from marathon number five. My training schedule was for a six-mile run and I stubbornly pressed on with that at the detriment of any future runs that week, or even that training cycle. All that mattered to me at that moment was finishing the run and doing all of those six miles. In my mind I had to complete every prescribed run if I had any chance of completing my marathon. This wasn't my first attempt at running through pain and hoping it would go away. In the run-up to marathon number two just one year earlier I had a run-in with a softball. It struck me in the shin during a match and soon after I developed shin splints in that leg. "Pah, shin splints, they're not a real injury. I'll just run through it." This did not work. After the first few miles of a run the pain would disappear, but the morning after it was back with vengeance and had me hobbling around again. As the pain got worse my runs got less and less frequent. I should have known better and I should have learned my lesson, but I hadn't.

Here I was training for my fifth marathon and making the same old mistakes. I got back to my flat three miles after the pain had started, surprised but thankful that I had managed not to fall over. I took some ibuprofen, donned a compression bandage and set up camp on the sofa hoping the pain would go away. When, two hours later, it had got worse I thought "it'll be ok in the morning" and went to sleep. And when, come the morning, it had become a piercing pain that shot right through my leg and made me wince at the slightest movement, I finally gave in and decided to go get it checked out.

I arrived at the minor injuries unit at St Thomas' Hospital as a man with chest pains staggered through the door and immediately I felt like a fraud. But a sympathetic nurse with a good understanding of running injuries took pity on me and had a look at my leg. "Do you have any idea what you think it could be?" he asked me.

"Well I've already had one diagnosis from a bus driver this morning who told me it's my back."

"Hmm, it's not your back."

"I didn't think so. I'm just a bit worried that it could be a stress fracture."

What I wanted him to say in response to this was "oh I don't think it's that". I knew enough about running injuries to know that a stress fracture would put me out for around ten weeks. That meant no running for ten weeks, no marathon training and a 'gradual' return to running after the ten weeks were up. Worst of all, no marathon. But he didn't say that.

"Yes, that is a concern. I could x-ray you but as stress fractures are difficult to see on an x-ray, it wouldn't show up right now anyway."

This was bad news. His advice was to take ibuprofen and to rest the leg for ten days. If it still hurt then I was to go back. I would spend ten frustrating days waiting to find out if my leg was broken or not and if my new marathon PB would have to be put on hold.

When I had first started running, a tight muscle, a niggling pain or a sore foot were a welcome excuse to get out of training. If I felt I had a legitimate reason to skip a run in favour of sitting on the sofa watching TV, I would gladly take it. But somewhere along the line, injuries became the enemy. They threatened to steal my goals and the fitness that I had built up. While ten days of waiting to see if my leg was ok or not wouldn't make any real difference to my strength or fitness, it felt like a prison sentence. I should be out running, not sitting on the bus. Once running has become part of your life, part of your weekly routine and part of how you identify yourself as a person, being told not to run can cause all sorts of feelings. I wanted tell myself that worse things happen to people than a stress fracture – that even if that was the case I would run again in time. But all sense of reason had gone out the window and I sunk down into a bad mood that lasted a few days. When I saw other people out running on my way to and from work I'd feel pangs of jealousy. That should be me out running, not them – it wasn't fair.

I became impatient waiting for the ten days to pass and wanted to know immediately if my leg was better or not. It didn't hurt to walk anymore so maybe I could chance it? But as I rushed across the platform to get on an underground train one evening I felt a sharp pain in my leg. It was a warning that I needed to be patient and wait out the full ten days, but it made me doubt that it would be ok after the running curfew had passed.

At the weekend I travelled home to see family. I looked at my training plan: I should have been doing a long run of 12 miles. I desperately wanted to be out in the sunshine running around the lakes where I'd done several long runs before each of my marathons, but this was off limits. Instead I got my mum's rusty old mountain bike out of the garage and cycled 12 miles as fast as I could manage. In London, the traffic and stop signs make it difficult to get much speed up on a bike, but as I cycled down miles of traffic free lanes and round the lakes my legs peddled as fast as they could – I needed to feel I was doing something towards my training, and I needed the endorphin rush that exercise brings.

At the end of my cycle, my legs ached more than they had in weeks. But it wasn't the same as running. All I wanted to do was run, to clock up some miles and put a big tick on my schedule. I went swimming, back and forth in the pool I swam my inefficient breast stroke, but this wasn't running either. I even tried doing yoga to keep my body moving and take my mind off my injured leg.

I made a plan too. If, at the end of the ten days, my leg was broken and I needed ten weeks off, I would get good at swimming. I would take lessons and get a new bike, a faster bike.

I would spend ten weeks getting good and swimming and cycling and then, when I was allowed to run again, I would take on a triathlon. I tried to stay positive and focus on what I could do rather than what I couldn't, but I knew if it was bad news I'd be no fun to be around for weeks.

When the ten days were up, I nervously put on my trainers and headed out the office at lunchtime for a three-mile run along the Thames. The first few tentative steps felt ok, and I wasn't in pain. I ran a little faster, stretching my stride out and it was still ok. I speeded up a little more, I overtook a pair of runners and I ran three miles without any complaint from my leg. I was back!

Every marathon I've completed has been threatened by the dark cloud of injury. While training for marathon number two, the shin splints that I tried to train through got worse and worse until I began missing runs and eventually had to take a break from running. As the race got nearer the goal I had set for myself of finishing under four hours looked less and less certain. But I was determined to give it my best shot. A week before marathon number four in Edinburgh I did something to my Achilles in the last mile of my last long run that left me hobbling around for days, unable to get up steps without pain. An extreme taper that consisted of just a handful of runs in the three weeks before the race and a couple of visits to see a physiotherapist worked on this occasion. While I may not have learned my lesson in terms of stopping running when something hurts,

I have learned to listen to my doctor, nurse or physiotherapist when they tell me to rest. So far, following their advice, doing the stretches they suggest and sitting on the injury bench for as long as they tell me not to run has allowed me to recover quickly. Sometimes the best medicine is the one that's hardest to take.

What I wish I had known then

What to do when injury strikes

There's two simple things to remember when it comes to injuries. The first is to stop what you're doing. So if you're running and something is hurting, stop running. If you're doing strength exercises and something is hurting, stop doing them. You get the idea. It may sound simple but as I, and countless other runners prove, stopping mid-run is sometimes a difficult thing to do.

The second thing to remember is RICE. RICE is like the mirror, signal, manoeuvre of running injuries. It stands for Rest, Ice, Compression and Elevation. Rest, as in stop running and rest; ice – get a packet of frozen peas or something similar and put it on whatever hurts, compression – stick a tubigrip on it if possible and elevate it – put your feet up.

When you start running or training for an event and increasing your mileage, you're going to get a certain amount of aches and pains. You're asking your muscles to do things they've not done before or, at least, haven't done in a long time. What you need to learn, and this will only come from experience, is the difference between normal aches and pains that we all get and an injury that needs attention. Anything that comes on suddenly should be viewed as the latter and you should stop running. If in doubt, see a doctor or a physiotherapist and get yourself checked out.

If you're told to rest for a few days this can be frustrating but listen to that advice. If you're allowed, do some cross-training: cycling, swimming, pool jogging – anything that will get your heart rate up but not put stress on whichever part of you is injured. If you're working to a training plan and worried that you'll slip behind, you can use cross training to keep your fitness up. So if your plan calls for a three-mile run, work out how long this would usually take you and cross-train for the same amount of time at a similar intensity. If it would take you 30 minutes to run three miles, get on your bike and cycle for half an hour at a similar level of effort.

Among all the frustration of not being able to run, of missing training sessions and possibly missing a race, there is one good thing that's come out of it. Sometimes training can become a chore and trying to fit runs in between work, sleeping and social commitments can seem like hard work. When faced with the prospect of potentially having up to ten weeks out of running it makes you realise that running is something you WANT to do. It's something to make time for, not something to be squeezed in to whatever gap it fits.

Most importantly, listen to the advice you're given. Your doctor or physiotherapist may not give you the answer that you want to hear – but it's important you hear what they have to say. My ten-day wait was frustrating, but I healed because I listened to that advice, I didn't make the situation worse. And once I was able to run again I had a renewed enthusiasm for it.

If injury or the advice you're given means you have to miss a race that you've been training towards this can be hugely disappointing. But it's important that you try not to see the fitness you've built up over the past however many weeks as being 'wasted' because you can't take part in your race. Yes, your race may have been the focus, but you've built up your fitness not just for this one day but for the good of your health forever and for future races too. It might be tempting to think that you can get round a race with your injury, push through the pain and then take a rest after – but you could do yourself more harm in the long run. Do you really want to risk future races and runs for the sake of this one that you're unlikely to perform at your best in because, after all, you're injured?

Fitness doesn't have an expiry date. Two days after your race, the fitness and strength that you've built up doesn't suddenly disappear – nor will it if you're forced to take a break of a week or two. A prolonged break may mean you lose a bit of speed or endurance but probably not as much as you think. Find a new goal to focus on in the future and shift your focus to working towards that instead.

Chapter 13

Where did it all go wrong? – facing failure

I'M at the start line of the marathon, only I'm in New York instead of Nottingham where I'm due to be taking on marathon number two. I start running but I'm going too fast and I know I should slow down, but I'm feeling ok. Then I reach for a gel, but I don't have any with me. I panic that I'm not going to be able to run any further and that I'm going to hit 'the wall'. I ring my mum (because clearly a phone was more essential to pack than gels) but she's not there. So I ring my sister and try to explain to her where to find my gels, but she's 100 miles away. I get off the phone but I don't know where or when I'm going to meet up with her. And then I wake up.

I was having a marathon anxiety dream. I've never had trouble sleeping. I've put in some valuable training over the years to perfect my ability to sleep soundly for a good eight hours most nights. Of course, this hasn't always been easy, but I've persevered and now I'm pretty good at it – in fact I'd say I'm in the elite category when it comes to sleep. I've even managed power naps in nightclubs in Amsterdam and Ireland. That's just how I roll. But marathons have been known to threaten my beloved 40 winks. My marathon anxiety dreams generally start about six weeks before the big day and have ranged from being at the start line in my pyjamas with no shoes to being chased by a dinosaur. On this occasion I was dreaming of the New York Marathon, presumably because I kept telling people that Nottingham is the New York of the Midlands.

My friend Rostam and I had signed up to run the Nottingham Marathon (or the Robin Hood Marathon to give the official title) together. It would be his first marathon and my second. We had looked at a long list of marathons and decided this one looked a good option – close enough to our home town that we could get some crowd support, in September so it wouldn't be too hot or too cold, and most importantly – it was pretty cheap. So we packed up our bags one Saturday in September and headed for a budget hotel in the Midlands.

Taking on your second marathon is a different ball game to tackling your first. If you've run the first with a modest but sensible goal as I had of just finishing with a smile on my face, you might give yourself a greater challenge, try and shave a few minutes off. It had been 18 months since I had done my first marathon. Unlike marathon number one where I had been content with just running all the way without stopping and finishing in one piece, the second time around I had set myself a goal time and had decided I was going to cut a massive 31 minutes of my previous performance. I wanted to finish in less than four hours and had been working from a training plan that promised to get me to the finish line on target. But training hadn't gone well and injury had meant me missing quite a few runs. Despite these gaps in my training, I was confident that I would get a good time and go sub-four when the big day arrived.

My subconscious brain, however, was worried that my target might have been over-ambitious and that I couldn't do it, and this was manifesting itself in dreams that I was back at school but completely naked or being chased by a dinosaur. Only I wasn't listening to my subconscious brain, I was listening to the bravado that had told everyone who cared to listen that I was destined to go sub-four and that had decided to run through shin splints because they 'weren't a real injury'.

One afternoon I was describing how my marathon training for Nottingham was going to a colleague who said: "Ah, that what it's like when you have a baby." I had forgotten that training for a marathon is actually quite hard. I knew that running 26.2 miles around Nottingham in September would be difficult. That fact hadn't escaped me. But I'd forgotten about the training bit being probably harder than the day itself. All those memories of solo 18 milers had been magically rose-tinted in my mind. I imagined that training would be one long romp across London a couple of nights a week, only this time (as the Nottingham marathon was in September) it would be sunny for my training runs rather than minus ten. What my colleague was suggesting was that in the same way that Mother Nature wipes the complete horror of pregnancy and childbirth from women's minds to trick them into going through it all again, my mind was cleansed of the reality of marathon training. But by week four my legs were starting to remember. Back-to-back runs are tiring, and it was going to get worse before it got better. I wanted it to stop but it was too late: the race was entered, the hotel booked and this baby had to come out one way or another. And there's no epidural for marathoning.

Rostam and I had made it through our training and to the start line in one piece and this was the hard part over. The race would be the easy part. Or so I told myself. But Nottingham was an unforgiving course and it punished me for every hill training session I had missed. The start, halfway point and the finish of the course were all at the same place so the laws of geography should dictate that for every uphill there would be an equivalent downhill. It didn't seem that way to my legs. Like the Penrose steps, the optical illusion that makes a staircase look as though it's constantly going up with no end, the first half of the race only ever seemed to be uphill. During the first half of the race I'd rigidly stuck to my sub-four pace, not slowing down for the hills even though the second half of the route was flat and could have allowed me to make up time. This had destroyed my legs and they weren't going to recover. Between miles nine and 13 the most boring man in the world was running behind me.

This is the sort of thing you can't train or plan for. He was giving some poor guy a lecture about nutrition for a good few miles before discussing how much he had earned at various jobs he has had and then going on (after we all had to step aside for an ambulance to get through) about how he'd seen a guy get defibrillated at the London Marathon. Did he really think any of us wanted that vision in our minds while running our legs off? Eventually he overtook me and I was left, again, to my own thoughts.

At the half way point, the 5,500 runners who had wisely opted for the half-marathon turned off for their finish, and a lonely 1,400 of us carried on for the rest of the course. And this was where it started to go a bit wrong for me. I made it to where my family waited excitedly at the 17-mile mark before my speed took a nosedive. My mum urged me on by shouting out: "Just look at that gentleman's bottom and follow it to the finish." The man she was referring to soon started running again, perhaps to get away from me and my lecherous stares, but I, however, did not.

Shortly after this the route turned onto a huge rowing lake that we were to run a lap of. The day before, Rostam and I had laughed nervously at newspaper headlines warning that a hurricane was headed for the UK. Surely they were mistaken. But as we turned onto the lake and hit a mile-long wind tunnel of doom it seems the weathermen hadn't been too far wrong on this one. I had to accept that sub-four was not going to happen. But once your goal has slipped away it's difficult to keep on keeping on. Sub-4.10 had always been the Plan B and something I would have been happy with, but this too was looking under threat. Everyone around me was struggling to keep running and those that decided to walk were keeping shoulder to shoulder with those trying to fight their way through the wind at a running pace. Sub-4.10 vanished into the distance too. From here it was a long slog back along the River Trent to the finish with some of the hardest five miles I've ever run stretched out in front of me.

What I remember most about Nottingham marathon though is not the wind, but the support. My family were the stars of the day and officially the hardest working spectators on the course. They made it to miles 17, 20, 23 and the finish to cheer me on, along with any other runner going past. And they did this all without using any banned substances. To be fair, though, I had given them a fighting chance of catching me four times by slowing considerably between these miles. But without their support, those wind tunnel miles would have been much harder.

Marathons don't accept excuses. There are no shortcuts and no miracles, you get what you deserve. That's the way I like it and that's why I crossed the line in Nottingham without my sub-four time and accepted four hours and 17 minutes, if not happily, then graciously. On this occasion, it wasn't on the cards because I didn't put the hard work in. 4.17 was a PB by 14 minutes, but it wasn't all I had hoped it would be. Yes, it was windy and yes, it was hillier than I'd planned for, but no excuses: my training just didn't warrant a sub-four this time around. I should have accepted this sooner. Instead I went through the hilly first half in two hours which meant a lot of suffering in the second half.

On the bright side though, the 14 minutes I knocked off my Brighton marathon time was one of three PBs I set that day. The first? Only one toilet/bush stop on the marathon course. Although this was the second time that Nottingham had been exposed to my bare rear end in the past couple of months after my skirt blew up while I was on a night out there a few weeks earlier (see 'Reasons why I didn't go sub-four'). PB number three is for the number of black toenails I got during the marathon – five eclipsed the three I got in Brighton. So it wasn't all bad.

As for Rostam, he finished in six hours and 21 minutes and had resorted to licking the sweat off his arms to try to get some salt into him and stop his leg from cramping. Six months later our friends Andy and Emma would be standing at mile 20 of the London Marathon with a packet of crisps waiting for him as he completed his second marathon to save him the same indignity. We got the train back to London together with a table full of the post-run snacks we had been dreaming of for the 26 miles we had been running, both exhausted but in very different moods.

For the past four months my life I had been focussed on running my second marathon and getting a PB that was under four hours. Now that was over and hadn't been the fairytale ending that I had dreamed of, I was at a loss as to what to do now. Yes, there would be other marathons. During a moment of taper madness a couple of weeks before Nottingham, I had signed up for a place in the Edinburgh Marathon for the following May. In less than a month I would get rejected from London Marathon once again, but I would agree to take on a place in Brighton Marathon that a friend would offer to defer to me. So that's how I found myself with places in two spring marathons with just six weeks between them. I should have looked at the mistakes I had made in Nottingham, let my body recover and then lace my trainers up and get back out there – build on the marathon fitness I had, not allow myself to go backwards.

I had two chances lined up ready to bounce back from this disappointment, I needed to approach this sensibly and make sure I got my sub-four time come spring. But that wasn't what I did. Instead I packed up my life, left my job and flew to the other side of the world for four months.

What I wish I had known then
How do you bounce back after failure and disappointment?

I wanted a sub-four PB marathon. I had talked and written about how I was aiming to go sub-four, but the conditions on the day, bad pacing, injury and not enough preparation combined to make that a story to be continued.

Putting failure to the back of the mind wasn't the way to go. Learning from what I could have done better and accepting the things I couldn't have planned for was. Lacing up my trainers for the first long run of the next marathon campaign would be a nervous affair.

Would I be putting myself through weeks of training just to fail again? Luckily when the time came I had company in the shape of my dad who came with me on his bike (and wearing my 'small' London Marathon reject jacket). As I shouted out my mile times we breezed through ten and a half miles to do a negative spilt and end up coming home at a net sub-two half-marathon pace. There was a long way to go before I would go sub-four – but I knew it would happen because now I knew what it would take.

It's not just races that can leave you feeling a sense of failure, any run or aspect of your training that doesn't go to plan can have the same effect. Planned to run four times this week but only ran twice? Feel like a failure. Set out to run five miles but stopped after three? Feel like a failure.

When I have a bad run or a bad race here's what I do: I ask myself four questions...

What could I have done differently?

What things were out of my control?

What can I learn from this?

And then I move on.

Chapter 14

Running away
from home

WHEN I was five my sister came home from
shopping with my mum to find me and my dad
watching *Lassie*. I was crying at a film about a dog
and she laughed at me. From that point on I didn't cry in public.
Falling over and scraping my knee or behind closed doors
was a different matter. But emotional crying in front of other
people wasn't something I did. As I crossed the finish line of
my first marathon I thought I might well up. I had been told
by countless people about how they blubbed like a baby as that
medal was put round their neck, but as I stepped over the line
and stopped my watch, nothing came. It was an emotional
moment and for five minutes I talked non-stop and thanked
every volunteer I saw for being amazing and helping me on
my way, but no tears of joy fell. The finish line at Nottingham
was a different mix of emotions: disappointment, failure, relief.
But still, no hanky was needed. Just a large drink and fast train
back to London.

Less than two months after Nottingham, I stood by myself
clutching my passport as I looked up at a screen at Heathrow
Terminal 3 and saw the words "Flight QF001 Heathrow to
Sydney". And I burst into tears. When I was little I had an atlas
of the world. I would spend hours looking at it, memorising
capital cities, tracing countries and colouring them in. It was
a child's atlas and alongside all the different continents and
countries it had facts and information about them. One of the

pictures I was fascinated by was of Uluru in Australia. It seemed to glow bright red as though it had a lightbulb inside it. I don't know why, but for as long as I could remember, I'd been drawn to travel to Australia. Maybe it was the fact that it was pretty much as far away from my home in the UK as you can get, or maybe it was the picture in my old atlas. But in 29 years, I had not made it there yet.

Running a marathon can do strange things to you. It can change the way you think and how you behave. These changes can be quite subtle and you might not notice them at first, but at some point you find yourself thinking that things you once saw as impossible or the reserve of a chosen few could in fact be within your reach. If there's one thing that I've learnt from running over the past couple of years it's that you can do more than you ever thought possible. That you have the potential to be physically and mentally stronger than you realise, and that hard work pays off.

A few years ago the idea of running a marathon was completely alien to me. It seemed like a superhuman feat and something that I could never do. Likewise the sort of people who could pick up a rucksack and head off by themselves to the other side of the world going wherever their fancy took them wasn't the sort of person that I could ever see myself being. But we can be whoever we choose to be. So I chose to be a marathon runner and an intrepid traveller, and that's what I became.

I had packed my life into boxes, left my job and was on my way to the other side of the world for four months. I had always wanted to go travelling but work, lack of money and lack of courage to go by myself had always got in the way. As I approached 30 I started to think that it might be a case of now or never. And 'never' scared me much more than 'now' did.

I'm scared of flying, but I got on the plane by myself and flew to 24 hours to Sydney, Australia. When I arrived I took a taxi into the city and checked into a hostel – this was the first time I had ever slept in a room full of strangers while sober – and fell quickly to sleep. Early the next morning I got up and went out up to the roof of the hostel and looked out at Sydney Harbour. The Harbour Bridge was almost within touching distance to my left and the Opera House shone brightly in the early morning sunshine in front of me. I was here.

It took almost a week for the jet lag to subside and the temperature to cool enough for me to venture out for my first Australian run. I put on my running shoes and ran down to Sydney Harbour Bridge, under the bridge and round Circular Quay to the Opera House then back again. It was early evening, still warm out and the lights of the city were shining. I was thousands of miles from friends and family but for the half an hour or so that I was running I felt at home. Putting one foot in front of the other, the simple act of running was such a familiar sensation that it became comforting. It wasn't so much a case of wherever I lay my hat, but wherever I lace up my trainers – that's my home. I ran in Melbourne, Adelaide, Brisbane and towns in between. There was no pressure of how many miles I had to run or how fast I was going, I just ran for the enjoyment of it and to see the places that I travelled through from a different perspective.

One morning I woke up at 7am in the stunning Grampian Mountains in Victoria. My trainers had been packed at the bottom of my rucksack which made them a hassle to get out because it involved getting everything else out, and the more times I did that the more reluctant my stuff seemed to be to go back in the bag. I had sat at dinner with a group of other travellers the night before. As I spooned a second helping of pasta onto my plate I declared: "I'm going to go for a run in the morning." I wasn't expecting to hear "I'll come with you" from someone else tucking into their carbs. I couldn't back out now. Running date made, when the alarm went off the next morning despite having drunk a few local beers the night before, it was difficult to hit the snooze button knowing that another runner was lacing up their shoes and waiting for me. So I too jumped out of bed and put on my slightly smelly kit which I had dug out from the depths of my bag.

We ran three miles through Halls Gap with the sun shining, the sky bright blue and the air crisp, passing nobody but a lot of kangaroos who looked on slightly puzzled to see people out so early. It's still one of my most memorable runs to date and, if not for the German traveller who was to become a good friend,

I might have backed out when the alarm went off and missed out on it. When I got back to my room I repacked my bag so that my trainers were at the top, to make running easier and make sure I didn't miss out on any other runs like the one I'd just had. It's difficult to motivate yourself to run sometimes and easy to find barriers between yourself and running. Remove as many of these barriers as you can, by repacking your own bag whatever that is, and make it easier for you to run.

From South Australia I headed north on a 24-hour train journey to Alice Springs. After 24 hours on a train, there were only two things I wanted: a shower and a run to stretch out my legs. If you've ever been to Alice Springs you'll be familiar with the distant sound of duelling banjos that follows you down the street as you walk anywhere by yourself. Needless to say it's not the most appealing town to run around and this comes from someone who is quite happy running round the seedier parts of South London. That aside, as I stepped off The Ghan train at Alice Springs station it felt as though someone was following me round with a hair dryer on its highest setting. It was 40 degrees in Alice. There was no chance of running.

From Alice I ventured into the outback and for two nights I slept under the stars in 'swag', didn't shower and drank beer from a can. I was living like a hobo and hobos don't run for fun. I walked round Kings Canyon, up Kata Tjuta and finally made my way to that big rock I'd dreamed of seeing since I was a child: Uluru. But there was no running. Then, on my last evening in the outback, still in the shadow of the rock, the clouds arrived and the wind picked up. It was time. Running kit now firmly at the top of my bag I whipped it on and headed out for a three-mile run. Tourists in air conditioned busses looked on confused as to why I was running. It was still pretty hot but the red dirt track was the perfect surface and the view at the end of the run of Uluru at sunset was pretty great too. After two months in Australia, running in all of the five states I visited, I hopped on a plane to Asia.

I'm not sure if it was my pale, freckly skin, my red frizzy hair or the fact that I was running, but I turned a few heads while out on my first run in Cambodia. After a long bus journey and a day rattling about in the back of a tuk-tuk, I was ready to pull my trainers on and head off for a run through the town of Battambang. The fact that I caused a bit of a stir isn't to say that exercise isn't common there. In fact the town has a communal, outdoor aerobics class in the evening that takes place across the river from the food stalls of the night market. This may or may not be a coincidence. In the Cambodian capital, Phnom Penh, I saw two local joggers shuffling round a park and along the river outdoor exercise gym equipment was being used enthusiastically by locals of all ages.

My route in Battambang took me through the town, along its river and back the other side, a total distance of about three miles. It shouldn't have been a taxing run – apart from trying to avoid being run over by a moped that is. The route was flat and the heat of the day had subsided. And yet for the last quarter mile it was hard. The air was thick from the constant stream of mopeds, tuk-tuks and other vehicles and the dust they kick up. If it wasn't that it was the decreased mileage and the increased eating I had been doing while away showing itself. The local dish, Amok, was too delicious to resist though. If this was, indeed, the case I would have more work to do than I would thought in preparation for the marathon start line when I got back to the UK. I started to think that maybe I should test out just how marathon un-ready I was with a race while I was away. A quick look online told me that there was a half-marathon happening in Bangkok three days before I was due to fly out of the city. The inaugural Thailand International Half Marathon had been postponed from late 2011 because of the floods that hit the country at the end of the year. It looked ideal. Apart from the fact that I would usually train for at least 12 weeks for a half-marathon, running three or four times a week, and that just wasn't going to happen. But I signed up anyway. Everyone knows one: those annoying people that turn up to the start of a race having done almost no preparation over and above pinning their race number to their shirt and then turning out a pretty good time. Why couldn't I be one of those annoying people?

Obviously training would be my Plan A for preparing for any race. But with just six days until my half-marathon in Bangkok I found myself in northern Thailand having not run in two weeks because the weather and a running injury had conspired against me. I say 'running injury' because it was an injury sustained while I was running but, in truth, it wasn't training but running away from thieves barefoot in the middle of the night in Vietnam. Once safely back in Thailand I had been practicing an alternative type of preparation for my race. This consisted mainly of cycling round some temples on a rusty bike, going to a couple of yoga classes trying not to laugh when I should have been going "ommmmmm", walking a lot and getting almost daily massages. Just in case all that didn't work, I visited a temple and got blessed by a monk. The Wat Phrathat Doi Suthep temple is on top of a mountain just outside the city of Chang Mai. I had been sitting in the temple grounds looking at a statue of Buddha when a Thai couple came and sat near me and asked the Buddhist monk to bless them. The monk took out a handful of sticks, dipped them in some water and began shaking them at the couple – and me. In his enthusiasm for his work he had included me in the blessing and I thought it rude to decline. He said a few words in Thai which I didn't understand, gave us some holy cotton to tie round our wrists and promised me "success in all that you do'" So clearly I had that half-marathon medal in the bag! Who needed training!

There are a few simple things that anyone with a few races under their belt should know about how best to get ready for race day. In preparation for the half-marathon in Bangkok, I disregarded all of what was sensible. It's wise to take it easy on the days before your race and keep your weight off your feet. Instead of this I carried a backpack the weight of another human on my back for the best part of a day while wearing flip-flops. You should try to get a good night's sleep the night before and the night before the night before your race – because everyone knows that the night before your race nerves will have you up most of the night. A 13-hour sleeper train from Chiang Mai to Bangkok was not the best place to attempt this. Curtains, surprisingly, don't cut out much noise from your fellow passengers and the shaking of the train isn't helpful either.

I arrived in Bangkok at 7am, checked into my hotel and then made my way to the race expo. I met a couple of runners who were also looking for where to collect their race numbers. Rish, a man from India who was in town for a conference and had decided to stay on for the race got chatting with me. He was in the 50+ age category and was planning to run the race barefoot. While we chatted he nibbled away on the biggest corn-on-the-cob I've ever seen. He asked me about my race times and told me that we should run together, and I agreed. I picked up my race t-shirt and my number, and managed not to have a tantrum when the official explained that the number on the front of my bib was my age grouping, mine displayed a big fat 30 thanks to my birthday a few days earlier. I asked an official if there would be toilets on the course and had to just hope for the best when her answer was to smile and walk away.

The alarm sounded at 3.45am the next morning, a time that I had previously only known as meaning it's time to get a kebab and find a taxi. This morning, though, it was a time to get my kit on and head out for a half-marathon. Running a race in Thailand is, in many ways, essentially the same as running a race back home: long queues for the toilets at the start, several miles of wondering why you signed up for this thing and first place is taken by a Kenyan runner. The differences being that it's hot, humid and those toilets at the start are of the 'squat loo' variety.

The Rama VIII Bridge in Bangkok, a striking mix of steel and concrete, marked the start and finish of the race. More than 700 runners lined up for the 21-kilometre race (the Thais preferring to measure their half-marathons in kilometres instead of miles) with more waiting in the wings for the 10k and mini-marathon, options which were looking increasingly more appealing than running 13.1 miles. My new running buddy Rish, who was taking on the course barefoot except for a pair of socks to keep his timing chip attached to, found me and we lined up. The course took us up on to the 'skyway', a highway about 50 metres above the streets below, and we headed ten kilometres out of the city in darkness before turning back on ourselves. It was 5am and it was already hot. The plan was to make hay while the sun didn't shine by running the first leg faster than the second.

The refreshment stops were being supplied by Singha. Usually I would have been disappointed to see a beer company handing out iced water, but as we reached the first stop it was one of the first times in my life that a free beer was the last thing I wanted. Half the water went up my nose as I tried to drink but the other half, and the ice cubes, went down the back of my shirt where they rattled for a kilometre or two. The next few water stations came thick and fast and, being used to running half-marathons marked in miles, so did the kilometre markers. Walking through drinks stations became my plan, but soon my legs needed the drink stations more than my throat.

We hit the half way mark bang on one hour (though I only know this looking at the chip timing data as I was running without a watch) but soon after I urged Rish to go ahead as he was looking for a PB. Around 14 kilometres I had to adopt a run/walk strategy but used my walking breaks productively by taking a few pictures and chatting to other runners. Then around 15 kilometres the 10k runners joined us.

With the sun starting to rise and the Rama VIII bridge starting to get ever closer in the distance, the reason for setting the alarm so early became clear – not only were we treated to a brilliant sunrise but it was getting even hotter now. I shuffled over the line managing to smile for the cameras in my slowest ever half-marathon time of two hours and 12 minutes. The plan had always been to treat this as a training run and a barometer for marathon training. What I hadn't banked on was a hug from Rish who had been waiting for me beaming because he had knocked seven minutes off his PB and was putting it down to my pacing in the first half. A successful day at the office and it wasn't even 7.30am yet.

Marathons number three and four were booked and in the diary, and I had eyed the dates nervously every so often as I had travelled round all these places trying to put thoughts of training to the back of my mind. I landed back in London on 29th February, and came back down to earth with a bump. It was cold, it was rainy and I had six weeks to get ready for the first of my marathons. The holiday was over.

What I wish i had known then

Running on holiday can be amazing: brilliant scenery, no inconveniences from things like work getting in the way and (depending on where you go) great food to refuel with. But it can be a right old pain the backside if your training schedule makes you feel guilty and your travelling companions think that a holiday should mean a break from training.

Before you go, think about how much running you want to do and then take off about 25%. Most good intentions for holiday training disappear faster than the free in-flight booze when a rugby team are on board. Doing 75% of your planned mileage while you're away is pretty good, and if you do more than that it's a bonus. Talk to the people you're going away with – are they expecting you to be on hand for rubbing suntan lotion on their back 24/7? Do they realise you'll be packing your running shoes? Have those arguments before you get on the flight so, if nothing else, you can ask for seats apart.

If you like company when you run, it's easy to find other people to run with. Runners are easy to spot a mile off on holiday. For a start, running shoes stick out like a sore thumb and thanks to airline baggage restrictions, you'll usually find runners wearing them as an everyday shoe. Make a run date with a fellow runner and you'll be less likely to turn off that 6am alarm – and you are going to have to set your alarm early if you're somewhere hot. So up and at 'em.

Think about combining two great things and indulge in a spot of race tourism. The internet is amazing for more things than just looking at pictures of cats – yes with a few clicks you'll be able to find and sign up for races in your holiday destination. Then when you get home enjoy wearing your exotic race t-shirt on cold miserable runs around the local park 5k.

And, should you find that running is a bit too much like hard work while you're away, there's plenty of interesting ways that you can cross train while away to keep your fitness up or keep your other half happy. Hire some bikes, do a few lengths in the pool or go on a long hike.

Chapter 15

All things in moderation – Achieving a good run/ life balance

I HAD a mouth full of poppadom when my best friend asked me to be her bridesmaid. We had been friends for 18 years. We went to school together, to university together, moved to London around the same time and she now lived less than a mile from me. Of course I would say yes and I was honoured that she'd asked, but my answer came with a caveat.

"Will I have to plan the hen party?"

"No, I want to do that myself."

"Then I'd love to!"

We hugged, we ordered our curries and we drank several pints of lager. When I boarded the plane to Australia I had made a promise that I would be back in plenty of time for the wedding and I didn't plan to miss it. "You will come home won't you? You're not going to stay there forever. I need my bridesmaid back, I miss you," came the regular text messages. Six months later, at my welcome home party that had become a belated 30th birthday celebration, my friend embraced me and said: "I'm so glad you're back. I need you to organise my hen party."

Either she'd forgotten my clause, chosen to forget it or assumed I was joking. I wasn't joking. I had seen friends try to organise hen parties, juggling budgets, booking venues, trying to appease 15 different people and ensure that the bride had a great time, and end up pulling their hair out in the process. I had spent the past four months with my biggest administrative task being buying a train ticket and the most taxing decision I had to make being red or green Thai curry today. But drunk on white wine and the hugs of those that I hadn't seen since the autumn, I agreed. Sort of. "Do you think I'm the best person for this? I'm not the best party planner – I didn't even plan this party. Helen organised it. Maybe you could ask her!"

"No, I want you to do it. You know what I like." How could I say no to that? Now my to-do-list had three important things on it: organise a hen party, find somewhere to live and train for two marathons. The prospect of getting back on that plane to Thailand had never looked more appealing.

During the two weeks before a marathon when you're running less miles (tapering) and your anxious mind is working overtime, a phenomena known as 'taper madness' can cause you to do all sorts of odd things. In a serious case of taper madness before the Nottingham marathon, I decided to enter the Edinburgh Marathon the following May. Then my friend Tim had to drop out of Brighton Marathon because his wife was due to have a baby the same week and offered me his place. Around the same time my best friend was visiting wedding venues and narrowing down a date for the biggest day of her life. I was aware that weddings generally happen less often than marathons and cost slightly more money to enter into, so I resisted making the request that she didn't book her wedding for the weekend of 27th May as I already had plans to run 26.2 miles round Edinburgh that day. Instead I edged my bets and agreed to take Tim's Brighton Marathon place as well as, that way I was assured of having at least one spring marathon that didn't clash with her wedding. Eventually the wedding date was fixed for 19th May. I now had a spot in two marathons just six weeks apart. In my overconfident mind, I would be killing two marathon-shaped birds with one stone (or getting two medals out of one training cycle).

The Nottingham Marathon had been a disappointment. But I now had two marathons lined up in which to nail my sub-four time. It was an ingenious plan and I couldn't see why more people hadn't thought of it. There was a pretty good reason why more people hadn't thought of it: marathons are exhausting, the training is exhausting and the recovery period after is something that shouldn't be taken lightly. If I was going to run two marathons I was going to have to take them both seriously, respect the distance and train properly for them. The training plan I followed was radical to say the least. It involved going travelling on the other side of the world for four months and running just once a week. I had this thing in the bag. Like most spring marathon runners I included a half-marathon into my training plan in February as a litmus test as to how training was going. Only my half-marathon was the one I ran in Bangkok two days before I flew back to the UK where I posted a personal worst of two hours and 12 minutes. This isn't the sort of time someone hoping to run a sub-four marathon should be posting.

When I touched down at Heathrow one drizzly winter morning, I had just six weeks until Brighton and 12 weeks until Edinburgh Marathon, so it was time to crank up the training. But not having anywhere to live in London meant a long commute from my parents' house 80 miles away to work every day, plus flat-hunting in the evenings. I was leaving the house at 7am and getting back at 10pm exhausted. Not running wasn't an option, so wrapped in a hoodie and two pairs of gloves because I hadn't yet acclimatised to London in March after spending the winter months wearing a bikini in the tropics. I ran in my lunchtime and made the most of my weekend long runs. Three weeks before the Brighton Marathon I moved back to London and was running laps of Hyde Park once more. I had run round Hyde Park week in week out in preparation for Nottingham, and being back there again made me feel like I was finally home. The plan for the Brighton Marathon was to run it with Katie who was taking on her first marathon. I had agreed to pace her round the course and would treat it as a long training run rather than a race. The plan went without a hitch and it was great to run over the finish line at four hours and 29 minutes with a friend who was delighted with her time. But 26.2 miles is still 26.2 miles and although I felt good at the end of the race and still had energy to spare, my legs and feet had taken quite a pounding.

Unfortunately the four key long-run weekends between Brighton and Edinburgh had been filled by Katie's postmarathon 30th birthday party, the hen party I was supposed to be the organiser of and the wedding that I was bridesmaid at. This was not the sort of pre-race build-up I'm led to believe that the elites follow. Training carried on regardless though, fitted in where I could find time.

For most of my marathon training cycle for Nottingham I conducted a one-woman experiment into the effects of beer, wine and spirits on athletic performance. My findings were that getting drunk on a Friday night and spending the Saturday recovering in time to do a long run on a Sunday morning left very little of the weekend when I wasn't flopping around my flat feeling the after-effects of either drinking or running. Luckily, for us runners who like a drink, the recovery process for both a 20-mile run and a night out on the rum and cokes is pretty similar: rehydration sachets, fried egg sandwiches, chocolate milk and a comfortable sofa. So I kept well stocked on these staples that summer. But I knew how the Nottingham Marathon had turned out. Too much of a good thing had cost me my goal time before and I was conscious of history repeating itself.

The hen party I planned went without a hitch – 15 women organised and negotiated round a wine and spirit tasting event, a posh dinner overlooking the River Thames and drunk dancing in a London nightclub until the early hours. The day after the hen party I didn't get out of bed until 3pm, the absinth, rum and wine doing their worst. But on the Monday, which was mercifully a Bank Holiday, I was again out running. This would be my last long run before Edinburgh Marathon and my sub-four marathon quest. I had no idea whether a sub-four time would be on the cards after the past five weeks of late nights and alcohol, so the plan was to use this last long run as a gauge of how well I was running and decide what a realistic time goal for Edinburgh would be based on that. I ran 18 miles through London and round Hyde Park with an average pace of eight minutes and 45 seconds per mile and I was feeling confident knowing that 26.2 miles of nine minutes per mile would get me a sub-four marathon. That confidence lasted until the final mile when running over the cobblestones by the Tower of London, a pain shot through my Achilles. I was less than a mile from home so I carried on running, took some ibuprofen when I stumbled through the door and hoped for the best. The next day I couldn't walk down steps without pain.

When I finally made my way north for the Edinburgh Marathon I'd had an extreme taper that consisted of running just four times in the three weeks before race day. The weekend before the marathon I'd spent the day carrying out my duties as bridesmaid for my best friend: signing the register, wearing four-inch heels and dancing until 2am fuelled by Jagerbombs.

There are lots of things that can get in the way of running, if you let them. Having a friend's 30th birthday party, another friend's hen party and her wedding in the five weeks before a marathon could have become pretty good excuses not to train. But they didn't. Likewise having a marathon to train for could become a reasonable excuse to miss out on social events and occasion, but this didn't happen either. When I had trained for my first marathon I pulled out all the stops, missed many nights out and generally ate, slept and breathed the marathon. This is what I needed to do at the time and that was what I was willing to sacrifice to the marathon gods. But this time round things were different, there was no possibility of shutting myself off for four months, so I found some middle ground.

I wanted a sub-four marathon. I had dreamed of it – seeing the clock say three hours and 59 minutes as I ran underneath it and feeling that satisfied feeling that I had put in the effort required and achieved my goal. But I didn't want it more than I wanted to be at my friend's 30th birthday, have a great time at another friend's hen party and be the last person on the dancefloor with her at her wedding. There would be other marathons, but moments like this only happened once in someone's life. So sacrifices would have to be made, and on this occasion I was willing to sacrifice my sub-four marathon goal if that's what it came down to.

What I wish I had known then

Alcohol has given me many things over the years, the belief that I can sing in tune and that the world needs to hear that voice being just one. But it regularly robs me of three things: a good night's sleep, hydration and the ability to make sensible nutritional choices. A vegetable samosa does not a proper dinner make. Sleep, hydration and a sensible diet are all important for anyone and they become more important when you're training for a race.

What I concluded though, in all seriousness, is that it's possible to train for a marathon without giving up your social life. But you might not be running to the best of your abilities. Your social life and family commitments are just as important as running and sometimes it's running that needs to take a back seat to seeing your friends and having fun. And you shouldn't feel guilty about doing that. We're not world-class athletes whose career, reputation and livelihood depend on the result of a single race. We're choosing to enter races and run because it's fun. Aren't we?

Be realistic about how much time you can give to running, how important other things are to you and find some middle ground when you have to. Sometimes you can have your cake and eat it, sometimes you can't.

Chapter 16

When a plan comes together – The Edinburgh Marathon

"**H**ERE for the race are you?" said the guy on reception as I checked into my hotel.

"Yes. Yes I am."

"Just the one person?"

"Yep. Just me."

"Ok. Well, here's the key to your room. Breakfast is from 7am and we'll have plenty of bananas for all you runners. Good luck with the race."

I had travelled up to Edinburgh by myself. Unsure how training would go with just 12 weeks from landing in the UK until race day I hadn't booked my train tickets or a hotel until pretty much the last minute by which time the prices were sky-high. I couldn't ask anyone else to shell out for a sober weekend and an early night in the Scottish capital followed by hours waiting around for me to finish a race. And, broke from four months travelling, I couldn't offer to pay for a companion to join me.

So I played down the race to those around me and figured that after four months travelling round the world by myself, I didn't need anyone holding my hand for a 26.2-mile jaunt around Edinburgh. As chance would have it though, my friend and former manager Kristy happened to be in Edinburgh that weekend visiting a friend, and one of Kristy's favourite pastimes just happens to be standing by the side of a marathon course shouting at anyone who runs past her.

After checking into my hotel and laying out all my kit for the next day, double checking that everything was there, I headed out for a short wander in search of some carbs and some water. It was around 4pm but the sun was out and it was pretty warm. I got an ice cream and sat outside in the sun eating it, enjoying my cold, sugary carb-loading. I got my phone out and checked the weather forecast for the next day again. You can refresh the BBC weather page all you want in race week but it isn't going to change a thing, and it hadn't. The weather for tomorrow was still showing as bright sunshine, no cloud, no wind and 24 degrees. This isn't what any marathon runner wants to see.

You can't change the weather, but you can prepare for it. So before I got on the train I had procured a very uncool cap and loaded up on factor 20 sunscreen. With fair skin and red hair, it doesn't take much sun to burn me, and I wasn't going to risk that. I reminded myself several times that I had just spent four months in 30+ degree heat so I should be acclimatised to these sort of conditions, and tried not to dwell too much on how much I had suffered in the half-marathon in Bangkok. I finished my ice cream and wandered back to my room, had a nap and headed back out to meet Kristy and her friend for some dinner.

As I walked across The Meadows towards the restaurant hundreds of people were sat out drinking, chatting and barbecuing in the evening sunshine. I envied them. They had beer, the whole evening to stay out as late as they liked and no marathon to run the next day. The three of us had dinner at an Italian restaurant and then we parted – me to head back to my room for an early night and the girls for a night out in Edinburgh. When I saw them next I would be at mile 23 of the marathon and it wasn't clear who was feeling the most sorry for themselves.

When the alarm went off the next morning I was already awake but still in bed trying to soak up every minute. I silenced the alarm and began a, by now, well-rehearsed routine of pre-race prep: I showered, I ate some porridge, drank a cup of tea and half a pint of water, I put on my kit and then sat down and tried to relax with some TV until it was time to set off.

My hotel was less than a mile from the start and when I set off about an hour before the gun went off, there was already a steady stream of runners headed in that direction. I put my headphones on and pressed play on my marathon playlist – I wanted to be in my own little world and block out the chatter of other runners discussing how hot it was going to be, how they were carrying an injury or that they hadn't trained as well as they'd hoped. I didn't want any negative thoughts to enter my head.

It was a little after 9am and it was already getting hot. Usually I would keep on my outer layers as long as possible before the start to stay warm, but there was no need. So I put my jacket and trousers into my rucksack, checked it into the bag drop and joined the queue for the Portaloos.

Edinburgh Marathon had an interesting duel start situation. The faster runners were starting from London Road at 9.50am while the rest of us started from Regent Road at 10am. I was in the front pen of the second start which meant I could see the start line as we stood waiting making me feel a bit like an elite runner. The announcer told us that a 78-year-old woman would be running her first marathon with us at which the crowd of runners applauded. Then we were ready to get going.

I had thought about my race plan a lot. Was I in good enough shape to go under four hours? Would the weather be against me once again? Should I try for 4.05 or something a bit more achievable? But I had run one marathon already this year conservatively, it was time to take a risk, aim for the sub-four time and see if it paid off. The worst that could happen would be a repeat of Nottingham and I would have to walk bit. In order to come in under four hours, I needed to run each mile in nine minutes and seven seconds or less. The first couple of miles felt good. The Achilles trouble I had been having seemed to have disappeared thanks to my extreme taper and my legs were feeling pretty fresh, but I didn't know how long this would last.

The route took us pretty much directly out of Edinburgh and towards the sea, which wasn't great for sightseeing but essential for avoiding hills. The route was undulating but overall a net downhill according to the elevation diagram on the race website. I must have been asleep during the massive downhill bit. It didn't feel very 'net downhill'. And as I had learnt the year before in Nottingham, downhills can punish your legs almost as much as the uphill sections. Two guys ran past me chatting about their pace, they too were aiming for a sub-four hour finish and the two of them running shoulder to shoulder was casting a sizable shadow behind them. I locked on to the shadow and their pace and tried to stay in that darker patch of tarmac as much as I could. Eventually the route turned back on itself and the shadow fell in front of them. I was back to being in the sunshine.

We hit the coast for the first time at somewhere around five miles just as the sun was starting to get really hot and making the sea look rather inviting. There was no breeze from the sea and the sun was so bright that it was causing mirages on the road ahead. The support from the crowds though was excellent, from kids with water pistols giving runners a soaking to those flouting the hosepipe ban that the country was under to hose us down. Any cold water was a welcome relief. Around mile 15 a runner in front of me suddenly stopped running and I lurched to the left to avoid going into the back of him. A twinge of pain went through my Achilles and my stomach dropped – not now! But 100 metres down the road it seemed fine again. Panic over.

The route hugged the coast for about 12 miles before we turned around at about 19 miles and headed back towards the finish. At mile 20 of the Edinburgh Marathon I was feeling pretty good, too good I thought. Had I done something wrong? Was I going too slow?

Everyone I had chatted to on the way round that was also aiming for sub-four seemed to be somewhere ahead of me now. But a glance at my splits every couple of miles told me I was bang on target pace. Then I started to slow down. From mile 20 my pace dropped by more than 30 seconds a mile. Running suddenly got tougher. Had I been on my target pace of nine minutes and seven seconds per mile all the way round I would have finished in three hours and 59 seconds flat. But this slowing between miles 20 to 23 would put me over my goal time by at least 30 heartbreaking seconds. I was in danger of finishing in a too close for comfort time of four hours and one minute.

It was time to dig deep and pick up the pace, so I speeded up. It hurt like hell, but I ran as fast as my legs would carry me. At 23.5 miles I saw my friend Kristy cheering and I put my feet down some more. I was overtaking everyone around me, it was hot, and it hurt, but from mile 23 to 26 I ran the fastest three miles of my whole race: 8.55, 8.56, and 8.50 which brought me onto the finishing straight with just a sprint finish between me and sub-four glory. I had run hard for the last three miles and done all I could. I crossed the finish line, stopped my watch and let out a yelp: it said 3:59.31. I had done it.

It always surprises me how in the space of a few seconds you can go from running as fast as you can to finding it difficult to walk. Clinging on to my medal and race t-shirt I staggered through the finish funnel to the baggage reclaim. I needed to get my phone and share the news. I rang my parents then texted Kristy and a few other friends who were waiting to hear. Then I sat down and, still beaming, I celebrated with a pizza and a pint of the special marathon beer from the Stewart Brewery beer tent. I sat chatting to two runners from Reading, one of whom was doing 20 marathons over the course of the year – Edinburgh was his eighth.

We compared notes from the race and shared pats on the back – I could finally sit out in the sun with a beer and enjoy the weather. I had wanted a sub-four marathon for a long time and now I had finally done it. Despite my painful feet that would take two weeks to heal well enough that I could put on proper shoes, I felt amazing.

What I wish I had known then

How to run faster

Do you want to know how to run faster? The secret to running faster is: running faster. You're welcome. In all seriousness we all, at times, think there must be a secret technique or method to make us run faster and we buy products, read books, trawl the internet looking for it. Essentially, if you want to run faster in a race you need to run faster in training, it's as simple as that. Oh, and you need to be patient.

I'm still no Usain Bolt or Paula Radcliffe and I'm still very much a mid-pack runner, but gradually over the past four years of running I've got a fair bit quicker.

My first marathon took me four hours and 31 minutes, the most recent took me three hours and 56 minutes and the next one, I hope, will be somewhere around three hours and 45 minutes.

I've also taken my 10k time down from 57 minutes at the first race I ever did back in Wimbledon in 2008 to 45 minutes. I've been asked a few times how I did this. Well, there's two things that have made it happen.

Firstly speed work – interval training and tempo runs make you faster by making you run faster. But you need to do it at the right speed. This is where a lot of people get it wrong. I use the McMillan pace calculator (see Resources section) to tell me how fast I should be running in a given session or a training plan that's based on your current speed will give you appropriate speed workouts to do. Before this I did interval sessions way too fast, couldn't complete them and had to take a day off because I was too stiff to run. So get the speed right.

Second is running with other people. Running with people who are faster than you makes you run faster. So whether you join a club (where you'll also be able to pick up some speed sessions with coaches), or run with faster friends or do some Park Runs, run with others and you'll get faster.

But patience is important too. There's no use in being a fast injured runner because you're not going to set any PBs sat on the injury bench. So take care of yourself, don't push too hard too soon, work at paces that are 'fast' for you and don't compare yourself to other people.

Pacing a marathon

As I rounded the final corner to the finishing straight of the Edinburgh Marathon, something finally made sense to me. I've read countless books and magazine articles on pacing your race, fuelling right and getting the right kit, hungry to know what I needed to do to get better.

One piece of advice stuck out at me: "A marathon is a 10k race with a 20 mile warm-up." It seemed like one of those soundbites of wisdom that didn't actually mean very much and certainly wouldn't help when the going got tough. If you've ever read the words "pain is inevitable, suffering is optional" in the comfort of you home and thought "this guy is on to something" and then been reminded of them 17 miles into a marathon when the wheels have fallen off, you'll know the sort of stuff I refer to.

But at that moment in Edinburgh it finally made sense to me. Logic says that running a marathon is hard, and therefore it will feel hard. But, you can't push hard and feel you're running to your limit all the way round a marathon like you can for a 10k. If the pace is right, the first half of a marathon, at least, should feel pretty good. I'd been feeling pretty good at mile 20 and thought I must have been doing something wrong – I hadn't.

Good pacing is about getting yourself to a point in the race where you can push hard for home – even if that means you're still going at the same speed that you started at. It's the balance between feeling good and feeling that you can't give any more. It's that 20-mile warm-up for a 10K race. And, maybe I'm late to the party, but I 'get' it now.

Chapter 17

Even runners get the blues – Emergency motivation

ON Christmas Day 2011, I put on a pair of running shorts, a sports bra and a Santa hat and I headed out barefoot for a run. I was in Byron Bay in Australia and my run along the beach happened as the sun was lowering in the sky and bouncing off the water. There was a huge tidal swell on the coast of Australia and surfers had been flocking to Byron Bay to ride the huge waves or, more often than not, get thrown about by them. Sports photographers had positioned themselves along the higher ground with their wide angle lenses pointing out to sea. There were plenty of pro surfers out there. The surf photographers, through their massive lenses and experience could pick them out but the rest of us just saw heads bobbing about and figures on surfboards. The sand was wet and firm underfoot as I ran along the beach and the surfers kept me entertained.

When I had started running nearly four years earlier, this is what I had dreamed of. I had wanted the Hollywood image of running along a beach for the sheer enjoyment of it, able to run as long as I wanted and not having to fight to take every step. I didn't want running to be something I just did until I got to the finish line of a marathon only to be forgotten again, I wanted it to become part of my everyday life. Here in Byron Bay I realised I had achieved that. If I was never able to run a marathon in under four hours or get into the London Marathon it didn't matter to me if I could have runs like this. Runs where I felt like a child again as the waves came in and chased me up the beach or when I'd let them catch me and I'd find the sea rushing up my legs. I felt like I could keep on running forever and forever would have been fine by me because I didn't want it to end.

All that I've achieved in running, finishing five marathons now and dipping under four hours, running a half-marathon in one hour and 44 minutes and a 10k in 45 minutes, all of that would be gladly traded in for more runs like this. When I first started running, the idea of it being something that came naturally, with ease, that was enjoyable and that made me feel like I was flying seemed ridiculous – more ridiculous than completing numerous marathons. But in time it came, and for that I'm grateful because not everyone can experience that.

About five years ago a good friend of mine called Helen started running. She began with a couple of laps round the park near that flat where we lived together and gradually built up to a charity 5k event and then eventually a 10k. I was impressed by her efforts and perhaps a little bit jealous at what she had been able to achieve. Like most people, she found the early days of running and trying to get fitter pretty tough. What we didn't know back then was that, unlike most people, she had an undiagnosed heart condition. Every so often we see the saddening headlines concerning runners that have collapsed and died during a marathon or half-marathon. Some of them will, like Helen, have had a underlying condition that they knew nothing about.

After many trips to the GP, a lot of persistence and a few trips to the hospital Helen was eventually given a diagnosis that would turn most people's lives upside down. She had to stop exercising and take medication for the rest of her life. Thankfully she had listened to her intuition that something wasn't right and hadn't decided to sign up for a marathon, because who knows what could have happened if she had. While all this was going on, I had began taking my first tentative steps towards becoming a runner.

Helen said to me one day: "If you ever do a marathon, will you run it for me?" And I, of course, agreed, although that seemed quite a way off at the time. A year after her diagnosis I came to run the Brighton Marathon for the first time – and there was only one charity and one cause that I would consider running for, so I raised £800 for the Cardiomyopathy Association.

Helen came to cheer me on in Brighton. She and her sister standing by the side of the route at miles 14 and 24 was a huge boost to me when I was feeling tired and sorry for myself. Because Helen has never once felt sorry for herself and however difficult I found those last few miles I knew it was nothing compared to what she had been through.

Sometimes it's a struggle to motivate yourself to run, to get out there and put in a few miles, but there are people who, for many different reasons, running isn't even an option. We're privileged to even be able to consider running. Remember that running is something that you've chosen to do, it's not something that you've been made to do. And occasionally there's a very special run just around the corner waiting for you to hurry up and get there. If all that hasn't motivated you to get your running shoes on, here are a few things I tell myself when it's cold and raining to give me that last little push out the door.

ONE

You won't have to run tomorrow. Think how pleased with you your future self will be. Don't you want to be that person tomorrow who gets to sit down knowing they banked a run the day before. If yesterday you had run, that could be you right now.

TWO

You're probably using up a considerable amount of mental energy debating with yourself whether or not you should run today, trying to find reasons not to and failing at convincing yourself you should do it. If you just went out for a run you could save all that mental energy and who knows what you'd be able to achieve with it. You might have your *Dragons' Den* idea. Or maybe finish a really difficult crossword.

THREE

You want to have run, you would just rather not have to do the running bit. So instead of thinking about the running bit, think about the smug post-run afterglow of sweat and how pleased with yourself you'll be for actually doing it.

FOUR

You'll never regret a run that you did, only the runs you didn't do. Well, maybe not never. If a dog bit you during a run you would probably regret going on that one – or at least going on that route. But think back on all the runs you've done. Have you ever got back and gone "well, I wish I hadn't done that". No, probably not.

FIVE

You can tell people that you went for a run. There are probably a few annoying doubters in your life who think you won't stick at this running lark and that it's just a phase. Stick it to them by going for a run today and then casually dropping it into conversation. It doesn't have to be a real conversation – ones in you head work just as well sometimes.

Epilogue

I WAS sat on the kerb by the side of a road in Hackney, East London, when I got an e-mail from the publishers telling me they were interested in this book. I was waiting for the Olympic torch procession to pass as the whole country was gripped in the midst of Olympic fever and it seemed quite fitting that I'd received the message that my own sporting achievements might be published on such a day.

The mantra of the Olympics was "inspire a generation" and while the weeks that we watched the Olympic and Paralympic Games certainly provided inspiration, that's not the only place that it's on offer. I've been inspired by Paula Radcliffe's achievements over the years, but I've also been inspired by members of my own family – my mum completing the Seabank Marathon when I was about ten and my uncle Steve doing London a few times – these were my first memories of anyone doing a marathon before I even really understood what a marathon was. When we see athletes doing remarkable things on TV it's sometimes difficult to see it as relevant to yourself. Seeing someone you know: a friend, a neighbour, colleague or a relative do something remarkable – run a marathon, cycle 100 miles, climb a mountain – brings it home to you that you too might be capable of doing something remarkable and this can be equally as inspiring as watching Usain Bolt.

I started writing this book in a park in Brisbane in late 2011. As I was travelling, I started with a pen and paper – it would have been easy to put it off until I got back from my travels and was reunited with my laptop but another thing I've learnt from running is that there's always an excuse to find to put something off until tomorrow, and there's usually a way round the obstacles in your way. I didn't start writing it because I had a unique story to tell or some insight into how to run a marathon that hadn't been though of before – I started writing it because I hoped my experience as just an average person who started out very badly at something but, with a bit of perseverance got pretty ok at it, would inspire somebody.

When I started running none of my friends had done a marathon so I blindly went into my training without anyone to tell me that how I was feeling about missed training sessions, not being very good at it or wanting to throw the towel in, was normal and that it would pass. Now a number of my friends have run marathons and half-marathons and I hope that I've helped them on their way to getting their medal and learning to love running. But my proudest moment was when my nephew who had come to see me do my first half-marathon a few years ago, this year asked if he could go running with me. I was injured at the time and unable to run with him, so instead I signed him up for the five-kilometre race that runs along the Great Eastern Run half-marathon every year. He and his dad completed the 5k, my nephew crossing the finish line with a smile on his face and clutching his medal with pride just as I had in the same race with my mum more than 20 years earlier. I hope that he continues to be inspired to run whether it's by me or by the likes of Mo Farah.

I'm writing the last few words of this book in Venice where I've just finished running my fifth marathon. I had hoped to be able to write that the goal I had set myself after Edinburgh of finishing my next marathon in under three hours and 50 minutes and therefore getting the 'good for age' status that would guarantee me a spot in the London Marathon had been achieved. It would have been a fitting way to end the book. On the day of the marathon, though, Venice was being battered by 30mph winds and rain. But the marathon went ahead anyway.

It wasn't the marathon that I expected to run. I was expecting to enjoy the novelty of racing abroad, soak up the atmosphere, enjoy the scenery and, with a bit of luck, collect my good for age time. But that wasn't how it went. At the start line I realised that I had already let the weather defeat me. I didn't want to be there, I didn't want to run and I knew that my goal time was not going to happen. As the clock counted down I knew something had to change, so while I shivered in my bin bag waiting for the gun I did everything I could to psych myself up for the race. I put my music on, jumped up and down and told myself over and over: "This is what you do – you run marathons."

Running a marathon is a mental and physical challenge and in Venice this was amplified. The 26.2-mile distance was made harder by having to run into the wind and being blown sideways by strong gusts and the willpower required to keep pushing on when everything was numb from the cold had to be even stronger. Although I hated every moment of the race and wanted it to be over, there was not one moment that I thought about quitting and I learnt something very important. Sometimes the number on the clock isn't the full story. Venice Marathon is the hardest race I've ever done and I walked away from it realising all over again that I was capable of things I'd never imagined. I finished the race in three hours 56 minutes and eight seconds. I know I have a good for age time in me but that's a story still to be written at another marathon on another day.

Resources

HAVING gone to Loughborough University where Sports Science is a valid degree and a purple tracksuit is acceptable daywear for a large majority of the campus population, I realise there is a lot of time, money and effort dedicated to the 'science' behind exercise. While you would expect top athletes to be utilising the latest research to help them train harder, longer, faster and win more, it was surprising to me that a lot of this science filters down to amateur levels too. And I can't say that I've been immune to trying the odd bit of advice.

I once read an article that said that drinking coffee within half an hour of finishing exercise can lessen muscle soreness the next day. Apparently it's the caffeine in it. Ice baths (as favoured by Paula Radcliffe) are said to have the same result. I've tried the coffee and I can't say I noticed a great deal of difference but I think I'll leave the ice baths to the pros.

What's most surprising is the amount of disagreement there is on some subjects such as when is best to stretch – before or after exercise, or both? What's the safest and most efficient running form? Heel landing first or landing flat-footed – or even running on your toes? I stretch after (although I still ache) and don't stretch before (mainly out of laziness), and I think I land with my foot flat. What this means for me – the world of running is undecided, but what I do know is that no amount of stretching, changes to my running style or ice baths is going to make putting on my trainers and running out the front door and putting in the miles any easier.

Next are a few sources of information that have helped me on my way to becoming a runner and that you might find useful too.

TRAINING PLANS AND TOOLS

NHS Couch to 5k
The NHS's popular podcasts are designed to take you from beginner to being able to run for five kilometres. The podcasts feature music and encouragement, and are free to download.
www.nhs.uk/LiveWell/c25K/Pages/couch-to-5K

Hal Higdon
Author of numerous training manuals, Hal's training plans cover everything from 5k to the marathon and offer options for novice, intermediate and advanced. His training plans are available free from his website.
www.halhigdon.com/training/

The Non-Runner's Marathon Trainer [Paperback]. By David A Whitsett, Forrest A Dolgener, Tanjala Jo Kole
This book and the training plan in it got me round my first marathon. It contains a 16-week marathon plan as well as a pre-training plan to get you from being able to run for a couple of minutes at a time to being able to run for 30 minutes.

McMillan Running Calculator
As well as giving you predicted times for different race distances based on a recent race, this tool will also tell you what speed to do various speed workouts.
www.mcmillanrunning.com/calculator

MEASURING A RUN

Websites
If you want to know how far your run is, you can use online tools to measure them such as:

Map My Run
www.mapmyrun.com

The Good Run Guide
www.goodrunguide.co.uk

GPS Phone Apps

If you have a smartphone with GPS, there are plenty of apps available that will measure how far and how fast you've run. As with all apps some are free or have free versions while others are paid for. A few examples are Map My Run; Endomondo; Runtastic; and Runmetre.

RECORDING YOUR RUNS

Tracking how far, how long and how fast you ran each time will help you see how you're progressing. You can do this simply in a notebook, or in a spreadsheet on your computer – or you might find one of these free online tools helpful.

Fetcheveryone
www.fetcheveryone.com

Dailymile
www.dailymile.com

Running Free
www.runningfreeonline.com

FINDING RACES

You've got your trainers, you can run a few mile but now you need to find a race to take part in. Where do you look?
Listings in the back of running magazines.

Race listings websites – such as findarace.com or runnersworld.co.uk/events.

Through your local running club.

Local newspaper.

Laura Fountain is a journalist, blogger, author and editor living and running in London. She's run eight marathons and is now training for an Ironman but just six years ago she couldn't run 400 meters. Laura is a UK Athletics qualified run leader and helps beginner runners learn how to run and, more importantly, how to enjoy it.